NEW YORK

Mets

FIRSTS

NEW YORK
Mets
FIRSTS

The PLAYERS, MOMENTS, and RECORDS
That Were FIRST in TEAM HISTORY

BRETT TOPEL

LYONS
PRESS

Essex, Connecticut

An imprint of Globe Pequot, the trade division of
The Rowman & Littlefield Publishing Group, Inc.
4501 Forbes Blvd., Ste. 200
Lanham, MD 20706
www.rowman.com

Distributed by NATIONAL BOOK NETWORK

British Library Cataloguing in Publication Information available

Library of Congress Cataloging-in-Publication Data

Names: Topel, Brett, author.
Title: New York Mets firsts : the players, moments, and records that were first in team history /
    Brett Topel.
Description: Essex, Connecticut : Lyons Press, [2023] | Series: Sports team firsts | Includes
    bibliographical references.
Identifiers: LCCN 2023037033 (print) | LCCN 2023037034 (ebook) | ISBN 9781493068777
    (trade paperback) | ISBN 9781493068784 (epub)
Subjects: LCSH: New York Mets (Baseball team)–History.
Classification: LCC GV875.N45 T659 2023 (print) | LCC GV875.N45 (ebook) | DDC
    796.357/64097471–dc23/eng/20230925
LC record available at https://lccn.loc.gov/2023037033
LC ebook record available at https://lccn.loc.gov/2023037034

♾️™ The paper used in this publication meets the minimum requirements of American National
Standard for Information Sciences—Permanence of Paper for Printed Library Materials, ANSI/
NISO Z39.48-1992.

CONTENTS

PREFACE

First, a note about firsts. They are so absolute—and are so much more enjoyable than lasts.

There can be only one first, and yes, there can be only one last. However, a last signals the end—it is final. That does not mean that lasts cannot be memorable, or emotional, or life-changing, because they can be. The last game ever played at Shea Stadium, for example, means different things to different people. However, the one thing that it means to everyone is that there can be—and there will be—no more games played there. It was the end. The exclamation point, of course, was when the building was torn down.

Firsts are more hopeful—they signal a new beginning. Yes, there can only be one first for any one thing, but following that first must be uncurbed enthusiasm for what can be—and will be. If you are the first batter to ever hit for the Mets, there will be thousands after you—you were just the epic and one-of-a-kind starting point. What comes after a first could be anything and everything.

This is a book about firsts. Specifically, firsts by the New York Mets, the team I have rooted for passionately for nearly 50 years. I don't, however, remember the first Mets game I ever attended in person. That lack of a memory really bothers me. In general, I have an extremely vivid long-term memory—almost photographic at times. I remember my grandmother holding me by the hand and walking to the ice cream truck when I was maybe three years old. Grandma would always let me get the ice cream cone which, inexplicably, had a gum ball at the bottom. It felt like the crime of the century when she used to say, "Don't tell your parents I got you this."

I remember the time my father slipped and was falling down an entire flight of steps in Section 221 at the Nassau Veterans Memorial Coliseum before an Islanders game because he was wearing some kind of clodhopper boots. I saved him that day, by the way, by grabbing the back of his coat and reeling him in. But no one could save the hot chocolates he had in each of his hands.

I remember the cherry crunch dessert my mom would make, and the mushroom and barley dish with the cream of mushroom soup and those crunchy fried onions. Delicious. I also remember the Mayor's Trophy Game that she took me to in the late 1970s with the Cub Scouts very clearly.

I remember always loving baseball and for as long as I can remember, always loving the Mets. When I was six, seven, and eight years old, the New York Yankees were the best team in baseball, winning three straight American League pennants and two straight world championships. I remember having a poster with a group of Yankees that said "Yankee Fever—Catch It!" I remember thinking—as an eight-year-old—that I did not want a fever of any kind and wasn't sure why it was relevant to mention a fever on this poster, but that Reggie Jackson appeared twice on the poster and that was pretty cool. I also loved that they misspelled Graig Nettles's name on the poster, referring to him as "Craig." Still, I was born a Mets fan and have come to learn the pain and fury that comes with that reality. I refused to trade my 1978 Topps Joe Torre Mets manager card to my friend Raymond, who lived across the street from me on Sterling Lane. Those 1978 Mets cards still give me a feeling inside today, nearly a half a century later. Something about the script team font still makes me feel warm and fuzzy.

I loved the Mets then, I love the Mets now, I always loved when my parents took our family to Shea Stadium to see them play, but I don't—for whatever reason—remember my first game. Over the years I have been to hundreds of Mets games, and I remember many of them for various reasons and for many firsts. I remember the first time I got to see Tom Seaver pitch in person—it was during his comeback in 1983. I remember watching a backup catcher's deep drive to center elude the center fielder's glove by mere inches when the Mets walked off the game and the playoff series against Arizona in 1999. That was also the first time that I remember the mezzanine level at Shea Stadium moving up and down thanks to the thunderous reaction to the homer. Remembering—and witnessing—firsts in baseball is a part of its glorious history. It bonds fans and it bonds families. Arguably, no sport has the historic currency that baseball has, and there is never a second chance to accomplish a first.

There are so many iconic Mets firsts, beginning with the team's inaugural year of 1962. Within the pages of this book, we will go back in time and remember many of them: from the very first Mets batter, to the first Cy Young Award winner for the Mets, to the first player to hit for the cycle, and so much more. Some questions will be easy, some will be hard, and some will be downright impossible to answer. Of the dozens and dozens of stories from the 1960s all the way to the 2020s, hopefully this book will offer some surprises to even the most seasoned fan.

We will uncover many forgotten memories from the days at the Polo Grounds, Shea Stadium, Citi Field, and from the road. Players, managers, coaches, broadcasters, and stadiums will all be fair game. From the first day that it was announced that there would be a New York Metropolitan Baseball Club, Inc., there have been many franchise firsts. In fact, the only first that will not be revealed in this book, sadly, is the first time that the author attended a game at Shea Stadium. That, unfortunately, will remain lost in time, paved over in the parking lot of Citi Field. The bigger question is, what are the firsts that you remember? Or maybe some that you have forgotten. I invite you to read on!

THE EARLIEST FIRSTS (1961–1966)

IT STANDS TO REASON THAT MANY OF THE METS "FIRSTS" WOULD HAVE come during their earliest years: 1961, the year before they first played in the majors; 1962 and 1963, their first two seasons in the National League; and the following seasons of 1964 to 1966.

The first set of questions in this book will all relate to the Mets' first several seasons. The first manager, the first hit, the first win—all of the obvious ones. However, it will also include some that will make you think—the first head groundskeeper, the first mascot, the first player who was traded for himself. Yes, you read correctly, the Mets had a player who was traded for himself.

Depending on your age, these might be blissful memories of a bygone era of baseball, a time where losing came second to the pride of having a National League baseball team back in New York City. A time before names like Seaver, Koosman, Agee, or Harrelson filled the dugout. Or, you might be younger and learning much of this information for the first time: how the Mets came to be, who the architects were, and who took the early punches. Only in 1962 could the Mets establish so many of their firsts. All of the major—and most of the not major—firsts in batting, pitching, and fielding by default had to happen that season. However, far from all of the firsts took place in that earliest of seasons. From 1962 through 1966 the Mets compiled a record of 260 wins and 547 losses. Still, there are stories to be told, players to be lauded, and firsts to remember—or discover for the first time!

Who were the first "Mets," before the present-day Mets?

To answer this very first of the first questions, we have to go back before the 1960s—way before. The New York Metropolitan Club was founded in the late 19th century as an independent baseball team. The club name, "Metropolitan," had previously been used by an amateur club that played in New York as early as 1858. However, this iteration of the Metropolitans, often referred to as the "Mets," played their games originally in Brooklyn and in Hoboken. After playing one season in the Polo Grounds, the "Mets" moved to Metropolitan Park in Harlem. That move proved to be ill-fated and brief, as the team quickly returned to the Polo Grounds, as Metropolitan Park was cited as "The Dump" by players and spectators alike. The "Mets" of the American Association returned to the Polo Grounds for games on days when the New York Giants of the National League were not playing. In 1962, when it was time to officially name the new franchise in Major League Baseball, its original formal name was the "New York Metropolitan Baseball Club, Inc.," a purposeful nod of tradition to the ballclub from the 1800s. Though it was nearly 100 years later, the 1962 Mets would also be playing at the Polo Grounds, an incredible commonality between the two teams. However, the current-day Mets were never referred to as the Metropolitans. As early as May 1961 it was established, as per Louis Effrat of the *New York Times*, that the team would go by the name the Mets. This brevity was reportedly appreciated by NYC newspaper headline writers, broadcasters, and fans.

Now that the team had a name, it needed some players. Can you name the first man to officially be a New York Met?

On October 10, 1961, the National League Expansion Draft was held for the benefit of getting the two newest teams in baseball—the Mets and the Houston Colt .45s—players for their rosters. The Colt .45s, who would later become known as the Astros, selected Eddie Bressoud from the San Francisco Giants. The Mets then had their pick. The very first player to ever be selected by the New York Mets was—Hobie Landrith of the San Francisco Giants. "You gotta have a catcher or you're gonna have a lot of passed balls," Mets manager Casey Stengel was quoted as saying. However, this would not be the catcher to lead the Mets for very long. Already on the wrong side of 30, Landrith was no superstar to be sure. In fact, when Landrith was sent the contract offer by the Mets, he turned it down because it was $3,000 less than he had made the year before with San Francisco. He told Mets general manager George Weiss that the offer was "totally unacceptable." Undeterred, the Mets sent the same exact contract back to Landrith three times, eventually leading to Landrith giving up and signing the deal. There was not a lot of leverage for players in 1961, and the $75,000 was the required minimum for all first-round picks in the draft. Landrith started the year with the Mets in 1962 but did not stick around in New York very long. In June 1962, the Mets traded Landrith to the Baltimore Orioles as the "player to be named later," completing a trade from a month earlier in which the Blue and Orange acquired Marv Throneberry. Landrith passed away just as the 2023 season was getting underway.

By 1962, the Mets had three minor-league affiliates, including the Syracuse Chiefs as their Triple-A team. Can you name any of the first three minor-league teams that the Mets had working agreements with in 1961?

This one is a tough one for so early in the book, but anyone who is of a certain age might remember that before the Mets stepped foot into their first spring training in 1962, they were affiliated with three minor-league teams—the Lexington Indians of the Western Carolina League, the Raleigh Capitals of the Carolina League, and the Mobile Bears—a Double-A team from the Southern Association. The Bears ended the 1961 season—their one and only season as a Mets affiliate— with a record of 61 wins and 92 losses, finishing eighth in the SA. They were led by a gentleman named Shephard Frazier, who batted .265, had a career-high 22 doubles, and drove in 57 runs. Unfortunately for the Mets, the Bears—and the Southern Association—would fold following the 1961 season. Unrelated to the Mets, of course! Or, was this an omen of things to come in 1962? For good measure, Shephard Frazier never played organized baseball again.

Who was the first manager of the Mets?

Hold on! Before you throw this book down and scream "what kind of nonsense book is this?"—we all know that you know that Casey Stengel was the first manager of the Mets. However, go back and look at the question again. The emphasis is on the word *was*, not the word *who*. Sure, Mets fans of all ages remember that it was the Ol' Professor who managed the Mets during their infantile years. The grandfatherly, likable, quotable manager has his #37 retired in the rafters of Citi Field and is one of the most beloved characters in franchise history. However, how many fans today really know who Casey Stengel was? How many remember that he started as an outfielder for the Brooklyn Dodgers way back in 1912? How many know he led the National League in on-base percentage in 1914? Many remember Casey as a legendary manager of the New York Yankees, winning an incredible seven world championships and three American League pennants in a 12-year span. Yet, few seem to remember he had three managerial positions before coming to the Yankees, managing the Dodgers and the Boston Bees—who would eventually become the Boston Braves. Before taking over the Mets as a 71-year-old manager, he had accumulated 1,730 regular-season victories. "There was nobody like Casey before him, and no one like him since," read the description for Marty Appel's book, *Casey Stengel: Baseball's Greatest Character.* "Casey Stengel was, for an astonishing five decades, the undisputed, hilarious, and beloved face of baseball."

Who was the first man to come to bat for the Mets?

Heading into the 1962 season, future Hall of Famer Richie Ashburn had built himself quite a resume. He had nearly 8,000 at-bats, led the National League in plate appearances four times, led the National League in hits three times—each time having more than 200 hits, led the National League in batting average twice—including hitting at a .350 clip in 1958, and led the National League in times on base five times. However, on April 11, 1962, Ashburn entered a much more exclusive club—actually a club for one. In front of 16,147 fans at the old Busch Stadium, Ashburn faced St. Louis pitcher Larry Jackson in the very first at-bat for a Mets hitter. The result? He popped out to center fielder Curt Flood.

Who was the first pitcher to start for the Mets?

As time goes on—and the years tick away—this becomes a more difficult question than it once was. You have to know your stuff to remember that Roger Craig started the very first game on the mound for the Mets, in St. Louis against the Cardinals. Things did not go well for Craig, or the Mets in that game, who went on to lose an 11–4 decision. Craig, an eight-year veteran, did not give the Mets much of a chance, as Stan Musial and Ken Boyer drove in runs in the second inning, and Bill White, Musial, and Boyer once again drove in runs in the third inning. As it turned out, it would be the first of nine straight losses to start the Mets' existence. Two of those losses would be charged to Craig, who went on to lose 24 games for the Mets in 1962.

Who was the first Mets player to hit a home run?

What is so remarkable about the 1962 Mets, a team that lost more games than any team in the history of the major leagues—even to this day—is that they had some of the greatest players to ever put on a uniform. Unfortunately, their greatness was achieved in uniforms other than the blue and white pinstripes of the Mets. The 1962 team actually had two Hall of Famers, and it was one of those men who blasted the first home run in franchise history. It came in the very first game in the team's history, when Gil Hodges led off the top of the fourth inning against St. Louis Cardinals right-hander Larry Jackson. Hodges, who had blasted 361 homers in his Hall of Fame career with the Brooklyn and then Los Angeles Dodgers, took Jackson deep over the left field wall at St. Louis's Busch Stadium. The home run moved Hodges ahead of Joe DiMaggio into 11th place in all-time home runs. By the end of the 2022 season, Hodges sat in 81st place on the all-time list with his 370 lifetime homers.

The Mets finished the 1962 season with a record of 40-120-1. When was their first tie game?

Ties don't happen in baseball—at least not during the regular season. Spring training games, sure—the 2002 All-Star Game, yes. However, on September 9, 1962, baseball's two newest teams managed to do something that is hardly ever done, in front of a frenzied crowd of 3,360 fans—they tied. The Mets and fellow expansion Houston Colt .45s started their game at Colt Stadium at 4:00 p.m. local time in Houston, mostly because of the broiling heat earlier in the day. The game had originally been scheduled for 2:30 p.m., but the 100-degree temperatures made that impossible. In 1962, the average length of a game was just over two and a half hours. Still, little wiggle room for the curfew rule which stated that no inning could begin after 7:00 p.m. Especially when you figure in the two rain delays. So this was not a case of the teams running out of pitchers, or playing 15 innings deep into the night. No, the Mets and Colt .45s were tied, 7–7, after eight innings of play, and simply ran out of time. The bottom of the eighth inning concluded at 7:07 p.m., and the ninth inning was not allowed to start. While the game was registered as a tie, with no winner or loser, all individual batting and pitching statistics counted from the game. Because this was a Houston-based rule, the Colt .45s actually tied two games in 1962.

What was on the cover of the very first Mets yearbook?

There were five editions of the 1962 Mets yearbook, and all of them had the same cover—basically. The cover, drawn by legendary *New York World-Telegram* sports cartoonist Willard Mullin, depicted a baby, wearing a Mets cap, a diaper, and spikes. It was said at the time that the "baby Met" was a caricature of Mullin's grandson, Ted. Oh, and one more thing: the yearbook cost 50 cents. As a comparison, the 2023 Mets yearbook would have set you back 18 bucks. The following season, an illustration of Mr. Met donned the cover of the team's official yearbook, but we will save that story for the next book, *Mets Seconds*.

When was the first season that the Mets did not lose 100 or more games?

Things could not have started any worse than they did for the Mets franchise. In fact, the earlier years of the Mets reverberate to this very day. Through the end of the 2022 season, the Mets have 4,652 wins and 4,988 losses. Simple subtraction, and apologies for including any math at all, tells you that the Mets are 336 games under .500. That means that if you are looking at things logically, the Mets will most likely never be able to reach the all-time .500 mark. Think about it—if the Mets won 100 games over the next nine seasons, they would do it—they would be two games over .500. Consider this for a moment: In their 60-plus-year history, the Mets have won 100 or more games four times—and never in consecutive seasons. Nine straight years of 100-plus wins is kind of a big ask. This all, unfortunately, dates back to the early 1960s, when year after year the Mets lost 100-plus games. In the team's first four seasons—from 1962 through 1965—they went a combined 194-452. That is 258 games under .500. It was not until 1966 that the Mets broke the 100-loss streak. Under manager Wes Westrum, the Mets won 66 games and lost "just" 95 for a winning percentage of .410. Hardly worth cheering about—unless it is the best year in franchise history! One year before names like Koosman and Seaver were even mentioned, the Mets sent pitchers like Jack Fisher, Dennis Ribant, and Bob Shaw to the mound. Each of those starters won 11 games for the Mets, whose offense was led by Ed Kranepool, Ken Boyer, and Ron Hunt. Hardly a contender, the Mets finished in ninth place in the National League for the first time—eight games better than the lowly Chicago Cubs. The Mets would lose 100 games in 1967, but would not do so again until 1993.

Who was the first Mets pitcher to throw a one-hitter?

On June 22, 1962, Houston's Joe Amalfitano—who was batting .227—lined a one-out single to left field. No big deal, the Mets were already 30 games under .500 and giving up a first-inning single to an opponent was hardly breaking news. Here is the only thing—the Colt .45s would not get another hit for the rest of the game. Mets starting pitcher Al Jackson completely shut down the Houston bats and allowed only two walks the rest of the way, as the Mets won the game, 2–0. Jackson, who entered the contest with a 3-8 record, was masterful on this night in the Polo Grounds, striking out nine batters. After walking Norm Larker in the top of the first to put two runners on base, Jackson retired the next 21 batters before issuing a ninth-inning leadoff walk to pinch-hitter Pidge Browne. Jackson closed out the ninth with three straight outs for the complete-game shutout. As with any well-pitched game, there are usually defensive gems to talk about, and this game was no different. In the top of the fifth inning, right fielder Richie Ashburn made a leaping catch to save a hit. Later in the game, shortstop Elio Chacón made a sensational stop behind second base and had the wherewithal to flip the ball to second baseman Charlie Neal who made the throw to first base. Following the game, *New York Times* writer Bob Lipsyte called Jackson a "complete master of the situation," adding that he seemed to get stronger late in the game with a "humming" fastball and a "snapping" curve. "For fans of the 1962 Mets, Jackson's star turn was a reminder that their ragtag new heroes were capable of playing tight, exciting, well-executed big-league ball from time to time," Kurt Blumenau wrote for SABR.org. "The feeling didn't last long. In the second game of the June 22 double-header, the Mets made six errors, Houston hit four home runs, and the Colts bombed the Mets, 16-3."

The Mets lost their first nine games as a franchise. Who was the first team that they defeated?

A win seemed unlikely as the 0-9 Mets prepared to play the finale of a four-game series in Pittsburgh against the 10-0 Pirates on April 23, 1962. Of course, of those 10 straight victories, five had come at the expense of the Mets, and only 16,176 people showed up to Forbes Field that day. Still, it would prove to be a historic game for the Mets and their fans, as the boys from New York defeated the Pirates, 9–1. Six players drove in runs for the Mets, including two RBIs by Mets starting pitcher Jay Hook. In all, the Mets pounded out 14 hits against four Pittsburgh pitchers, and they could put the fear of going 0-162 behind them. Instead, they finished with what is still the worst record in the history of baseball, going 40-120, 60 1/2 games behind the first-place San Francisco Giants.

What Mets pitcher allowed the first home run against the Orange and Blue?

Despite giving up 11 runs in their first-ever game to the St. Louis Cardinals and then another four to the Pittsburgh Pirates in game two, it was not until the third game in franchise history that a Mets pitcher would give up a home run. That honor—or lack of honor—like so many others, went to Al Jackson. In the second inning of that third game, Bill Mazeroski went deep. Not known for his power, per se—despite his legendary homer that ended the 1960 World Series—the Pittsburgh second baseman did reach double-digits in home runs in six seasons, including the 1962 campaign, during which he hit 14 dingers. Of course, this one, against Jackson and the Mets, was his first of the season and the first ever to be hit against the New York Mets.

Al Jackson was involved with several firsts in Mets history, including allowing the first home run hit against the franchise. On the bright side, he was the first Met to pitch a one-hitter.
JAY PUBLISHING VIA TRADINGCARDDB.COM, PUBLIC DOMAIN, VIA WIKIMEDIA COMMONS

When did the Mets turn their first triple play?

OK, this is a really tough one because you would either need to remember the 1962 season extremely well, or just be perhaps the most knowledgeable Mets fan of all time. The first triple play turned by the Mets came on May 30, 1962, at the Polo Grounds against the Los Angeles Dodgers. In the top of the sixth inning, with runners on first and second and no one out, Willie Davis of the Dodgers lined out to Mets shortstop Elio Chacón, who made a leaping catch and threw to second baseman Charlie Neal to double up Maury Wills. Neal then wheeled around and fired a laser to first baseman Gil Hodges, who caught Jim Gilliam lingering off of first base. It was a 6-4-3 triple play—and if you got that one, wow!

Who was the first mascot for the Mets?

OK, let's get this out of the way immediately—it was not Mr. Met. Nope, the huge-headed Mr. Met was first introduced to the world as a drawing on the covers of the 1963 Mets yearbook and programs. There was no actual Mr. Met mascot, however, until 1964. It wasn't Mettle the Mule, who grazed beyond the outfield fence near the Mets bullpen during the 1979 season. No, the Mets' first mascot actually was short-lived and debuted the year that the team did. His name—Homer the Dog, a cute little beagle who often held signs rooting the Mets on in his mouth. However, Homer could not really produce the way it was advertised that he would.

In 2012, *New York Times* writer Richard Sandomir wrote of Homer's weaknesses from back in 1962: "Manager Casey Stengel hated him and refused to let the beagle sit on the Mets bench. Homer was supposed to celebrate a Mets home run by running the bases at the Polo Grounds. According to Roger Angell's book *Game Time*, Homer performed well in rehearsals, but in his first real test he touched first base and second, then took a detour and raced to center field. He had to be wrangled by 'three fielders, two ushers and the handler,' according to the book."

Homer was soon fired.

What was the first official cola of the Mets?

Being the "official" anything in baseball did not really become a thing until more recent years. However, there were exceptions, as Rheingold owned the spot under the Polo Grounds scoreboard and then the Shea Stadium scoreboard to stake a claim as the official beer of the Mets, despite the fact that multiple brands of beer were sold in the stadium. When it comes to soda, however, typically only one brand is sold in a given stadium. For years—on and off between 1962 and the 1970s—Royal Crown Cola, better known as RC, staked a claim as the official cola of the Mets. By the 1990s, the Mets had graduated to Pepsi, and following their trip to the 2015 World Series, the Mets broke into the majors by renaming their Pepsi Porch the Coca-Cola Corner. For me, there has been no greater acquisition by the Mets than the 2016 pickup of Diet Coke. However, what is interesting is that despite claiming to be the official cola of the Mets, Royal Crown did not have any advertisements posted at the Polo Grounds. Coca-Cola, however, had a huge billboard in right-center field. Fans of a certain age might actually know the definitive answer to this question, but it is safe to say that the taps at the Polo Grounds have long run dry. Was it Coca-Cola that was served in that very first season at Mets games? Was it RC? The Mets only averaged just over 11,000 fans per home game that season, so finding someone who knows might be harder than finding an ice-cold RC these days!

Who was the first Mets player to be traded for himself?

Harry Chiti. There is no use in keeping anyone in suspense. The odds are you've never heard of him, and the details are much more interesting than the actual name. It all started in April 1962 when the Mets purchased Chiti, a 12-year veteran and catcher, from the Cleveland Indians for a player to be named later. Chiti had spent time during his career with the Chicago Cubs and Kansas City Athletics and was traded to the Mets before ever playing a game for Cleveland. Chiti appeared in 15 games for the Mets in 1962, batting just .195, making it clear that he was not the right fit in New York. So, on June 15, the Mets sent Chiti back to Cleveland as the player to be named later in the deal that had brought him to the Mets in the first place. He never played in the majors again.

Who hit the first grand slam home run for the Mets?

After spending eight seasons in the New York Yankees' minor-league system, Rod Kanehl was picked by the Mets in the 1962 minor-league draft. He made the Mets out of spring training because he was familiar to manager Casey Stengel, whom Kanehl had impressed while he was in the Yankees' farm system a few years earlier. Despite not being a power hitter and only hitting four home runs throughout the entire 1962 season, Kanehl smashed the first grand slam in franchise history on July 6, 1962, in a 10–2 win over St. Louis. He hit the grand slam off of St. Louis pitcher Bobby Shantz in the bottom of the eighth inning at the Polo Grounds. Kanehl had just a three-year career in the majors, all with the Mets, and homered just six times in the three years combined. "Baseball is a lot like life," Kanehl is quoted to have said, "the line drives are caught, the squibbles go for base hits. It's an unfair game." What's not unfair is that Kanehl's grand salami got him a mention in a Mets history book about firsts.

Who was the first pitcher credited with a victory for the Mets?

On April 23, 1962, the Mets were looking for a win—any win. They had played nine games and they had lost nine games and things were starting to get stressful. While history remembers the 1962 Mets as Casey Stengel's bunch of lovable losers, these were professional baseball players—mostly veterans—who were not laughing. "We had a bunch of guys who knew what they're doing," one Mets starter said many years later. "It was just a matter of time before we were going to win a game." That time was April 23 against the 10-0 Pittsburgh Pirates, and the pitcher was the man who said those words—righty starter Jay Hook. "The Pirates were a really good team," Hook remembered, "and we got out ahead of them. That made it a little easier." After being handed an early 2–0 lead, Hook himself slapped a two-run single to give the Mets a 4–0 advantage. Was this really the night? Were the Mets going to win a ballgame? It was, as Hook did his job on the mound, as well as the plate, giving up just one run and scattering five hits in the Mets' 9–1 victory. The Mets would go on to lose seven of their next nine games and lose a still-record 120 games on the season, but for one night—and a few others—the Mets were victors.

What were the first official team colors of the Mets?

If you are thinking that for as far back as you can remember the Mets have been Orange and Blue, then you are remembering far back enough. But the choice of colors was not just some fashion statement the Mets wanted to make when they burst on the scene to lose 120 games in 1962. From the start, the Mets wanted to pay homage to the Brooklyn Dodgers and New York Giants, taking the Dodger Blue and Giants' orange interlocking "NY" insignia on their caps. The thing that is always a little strange about this homage is—despite New York National League fans wanting to pay tribute to their old teams of yesteryear—those very old teams were still playing elsewhere in the National League. The Los Angeles Dodgers were still wearing their iconic Dodger Blue—they just changed the "B" for Brooklyn on their caps to an interlocking "LA." The Giants kept their orange insignia, but traded the "NY" for an "SF." It seems odd in the grand scheme of things that the new Mets would find it necessary to pay tribute, or homage, or whatever you would like to call it, to the two teams that left so many fans in New York with no team. Those same Dodgers and Giants stormed through those early Mets teams, probably chuckling from their dugouts thinking, "Oh look, they took our colors, cute." Still, the Orange and Blue remain the official Mets colors, despite the introduction—and reintroduction—of black as an alternate color. The Mets of the late 1990s and early 2000s, such as Mike Piazza, Al Leiter, and Edgardo Alfonzo, were known for playing—and winning—in black jerseys, and in 2021 those uniforms made a return for Friday night games.

What Mets pitcher started the tradition—a now everyday occurrence—of a starting pitcher warming up in the bullpen before his start, instead of out on the mound?

In October 1963, the Mets took part in a special expansion draft—a second bite at the apple, as it were, for the Mets and Houston Colt .45s, who did not reap many fortunes from the original 1961 expansion draft.

Each team was required to make four players available. In the first round, the Mets took a player by the name of Bill Haas, who never made it to the majors. However, in the second round, they selected pitcher Jack Fisher, who had spent five years in the bigs already for the Baltimore Orioles and San Francisco Giants. Fisher, who was set to make his very first start for the Mets at Shea Stadium in the 1964 opener, became overwhelmed by the crowd noise and general hysteria from the 50,000-plus screaming fans at Shea. He went to manager Casey Stengel to ask if he could warm up for the game in the bullpen, instead of on the mound, or in front of the dugout—where pitchers had historically warmed up. Stengel agreed and a new era was started. "It was a crazy crowd," Fisher recalled years later to the Mets website. "With the World's Fair going on and the first game at Shea, there was just a tremendous buzz. The fans were really crazy around our dugout. I went to Casey [Stengel] and told him I really couldn't concentrate with all the fuss. I asked if I could go get a little peace and quiet in the bullpen. He said 'by all means.'" After the game, Fisher told sportswriters why he felt he needed to be out in the bullpen beyond the right field fence. "I could actually feel the sound waves hitting me on the chest," he said of the game that day.

Who was the first opposing player to hit three home runs in a single game against the Mets?

On July 8, 1962—just four months before his 42nd birthday—the man they called "The Man" took Mets pitching deep three times in one game: an impressive feat for any player, a really impressive feat for a 41-year-old. Then again, Stan Musial wasn't just any 41-year-old. "Trouble with the Amazin' Mets isn't that they have old ballplayers," the *New York Daily News* exclaimed. "It's that they don't have any old ballplayers named Musial." Musial wasted little time against Mets starting pitcher Jay Hook, as the Cardinals great hit back-to-back home runs with teammate Bill White in the first inning. In the top of the fourth inning, Musial sent a long home run to right field to give St. Louis a 9–0 lead. He then led off the seventh with a second home run to right field—and his third overall in the contest, which the Cardinals went on to win, 15–1.

When was the first time the Mets won a home opener?

Through the 2023 season, the Mets have the best winning percentage in home openers by a very wide margin. That is even more impressive when you consider that for the first six seasons of their existence, home openers did not go well. In 1962, the Mets lost their home opener to the Pittsburgh Pirates at the Polo Grounds, 4–3; in 1963, the Mets lost their home opener to the St. Louis Cardinals at the Polo Grounds, 7–0; in 1964, the Mets lost their home opener to the Pittsburgh Pirates at Shea Stadium, 4–3; in 1965, the Mets lost their home opener to the Los Angeles Dodgers at Shea Stadium, 6–1; in 1966, the Mets lost their home opener to the Atlanta Braves at Shea Stadium, 3–2; and in 1967, the Mets lost their home opener to the Pittsburgh Pirates at Shea Stadium, 6–3. Finally, in 1968, things changed. On April 17, in front of 53,079 fans at Shea Stadium, rookie pitcher Jerry Koosman and the Mets shut out the San Francisco Giants, 3–0. Koosman was masterful, including getting out of a bases-loaded, no-out jam in the top of the first inning with Willie Mays at the plate. "I was thinking that Mays was a tough hitter," Koosman told reporters following the game about striking out the man who had 565 homers on his resume to date. "I wasn't scared though." He gave up just seven singles on the afternoon. Given that they lost their first six home openers and nine of their first 10 home openers, the Mets' 41-21 overall record in home openers in their first 62 years and the .661 winning percentage that translates to is quite astounding.

Who got the first base hit for the Mets?

On October 8, 1961, the day after the World Series, the National League held its Expansion Draft to fill the rosters for the Mets and Houston Colt .45s. "On paper it read like any other league announcement," Jimmy Breslin wrote in his book on the 1962 Mets, *Can't Anybody Here Play This Game?* "But it was really robbery in the daytime." Instead of having legitimate players to choose from, as was the case in the Expansion Draft one year earlier, the Mets and Colt .45s could only select from the ranks of aging veterans, utility players, and journeymen, who would have most likely been released to make room for protected minor leaguers in December. So, with the eighth pick in the draft, the

In addition to being the first Met to win a home opener, Jerry Koosman later became the first pitcher to start on Opening Day for the Mets after Tom Seaver had done so for 10 straight seasons.

Mets selected Cincinnati veteran Gus Bell. Bell had played 12 years in the majors at that point and was a four-time All-Star. However, he was now 33, beaten down, and was a shell of the player he had once been, so much so that the Mets would send Bell to Milwaukee in May 1962. However, he was there for the start of the season, batting fifth and playing right field for the Mets in the opener against St. Louis. After Cardinals starter Larry Jackson retired the first four Mets ever to come to bat—Richie

Ashburn, Felix Mantilla, Charlie Neal, and Frank Thomas—Bell stepped to the plate. His line-drive single to center field proved to be significant in the annals of Mets history, as that would always be the first-ever base hit by a New York Mets batter. It was one of only 15 hits Bell would get as a member of the Mets. After being traded to Milwaukee in May, he went on to hit .285 for the Braves in what would be his last season of consequence in the big leagues. His grandson, Mike Bell, briefly played in the Mets' minor-league system in the late 1990s. Of course, his son Buddy and grandson David also spent many years in baseball as players and coaches.

What was the Mets' first radio network?

In 1962, when the Mets debuted in the National League, their games were not broadcast on the former flagship station of the New York Giants, which was WMCA, or the Brooklyn Dodgers, which was WMGM. The Yankees games, at the time, were broadcast on WINS. So when the Mets' trio of Bob Murphy, Ralph Kiner, and Lindsey Nelson were heard that very first season, fans had to tune to WABC, 770 AM. WABC was—and is—one of the country's oldest radio stations, signing on for the first time in October 1921. In 1962, WINS was the number one music station in New York City, while WABC barely ranked in the top 10. Fortunately for WABC, the other Top 40 outlets could not be heard as well in more distant New York and New Jersey suburbs, since WINS, WMGM, and WMCA were all directional stations. WABC, with its 50,000-watt nondirectional signal, had the advantage of being heard in places west, south, and northwest of New York City, a huge chunk of the growing suburban population, allowing them to hear the Mets. In fact, due to its strong signal, the station could be heard easily over 100 miles away. If only the Mets could have had some more hits for their listeners. Get it?

Who was the first Mets batter to hit for the cycle?

One of the things that had plagued the New York Mets for the first 50 years of their existence was that they had never had a pitcher throw a no-hitter. Known as a pitching-rich organization since the late

1960s—Seaver, Ryan, Koosman, Matlack, Gooden, Darling, Cone, and on and on—no one had been able to throw a no-hitter, at least for the Mets. Almost equally as rare as the no-hitter in baseball is the cycle. Although a tad more common than the pitching feat, it is still quite an accomplishment for a batter to get a single, double, triple, and home run in the same ballgame. The Mets, who now of course have two no-hitters to their credit through the 2022 season, also have 11 cycles to their credit. The most recent cycle was hit on June 6, 2022, when Eduardo Escobar did the deed against the San Diego Padres, driving in six runs along the way. However, we now know Escobar was the 11th in franchise history. The first actually took place way back in 1963, the Mets' second season. On August 7, the Mets were a paltry 34-77 and facing the St. Louis Cardinals at the Polo Grounds. It was on that day that the 9,977 fans in attendance watched leadoff hitter Jim Hickman, a second-year out-fielder, go 4-for-5—not only hitting for the cycle, but doing it in order. He singled in the first, doubled in the second, and drove in a run with an RBI triple in the fourth. When he came to bat to lead off in the bottom of the sixth inning, he needed a home run to finish off his magical day. Batting against St. Louis reliever Barney Shultz, a 6-foot-2 right-hander, Hickman blasted a solo homer off a knuckleball and sent it out of the park in left field. "Needless to say, this was Jim's most memorable day in the majors," wrote Jim McCulley in the *New York Daily News*. Not only was Hickman the first Mets player to hit for the cycle, but he became just the sixth man in major-league history to do so as a "natural" cycle. "As of the end of the 2019 season, a total of 14 players had hit for a natural cycle," wrote Mike Huber for SABR. For the curious, or the insane, the other Mets cycles were hit by Tommie Agee (1970), Mike Phillips (1976), Keith Hernandez (1985), Kevin McReynolds (1989), Alex Ochoa (1996), John Olerud (1997), Eric Valent (2004), José Reyes (2006), Scott Hairston (2012), and—as previously mentioned—Eduardo Escobar (2022).

When was the first Mets-Yankees Mayor's Trophy Game?

The Mayor's Trophy Game—originally played by the New York Yankees and New York Giants—began in 1946 as a way to raise money for New York City's Amateur Baseball Federation, which included sand-lot baseball programs. Of course, the game became extinct when the Dodgers and Giants left New York following the 1958 season. It was revived during the Mets second season of play—in 1963—when they defeated the Yankees, 6–2. The winning pitcher for the Mets that evening at Yankee Stadium was actually Jay Hook, who also was the first-ever winning pitcher for the Mets in a regular-season game one year earlier. The two New York baseball teams played 19 years in a row, but did so for the last time in 1983 due to a lack of interest from both franchises. One interesting postscript of the Mayor's Trophy Game was unveiled by writer Jim Snedeker on the Ultimate Mets Database website. Snedeker wondered what had become of the impressive-looking Mayor's Trophy Game trophy. After all, without the trophy, what was there to celebrate with after the win? The trophy is in the name of the event! There was actually more than one trophy, as it seemed to keep falling apart along the way, leading to new replicas being created. But where is the latest, which was won in 1983 by the Yankees? "The Yankees do not have it. Neither do the Mets. The truth is, no one knows where it is," Snedeker wrote. "It turns out that after each game, the trophy would be paraded around by the winning team for a suitable period and then returned to New York City Hall, its permanent home during the offseason. So, if the Mayor's Trophy does indeed still exist, it is most likely sitting in a crate deep in the bowels of some big government building. That location and the last time it saw the light of day are unknown."

Who was the first Mets All-Star Game starter?

On July 7, 1964, more than 50,000 fans jammed into the brand-new Shea Stadium to watch the Midsummer Classic. The 1964 All-Stars included legendary names like Mickey Mantle, Brooks Robinson, Tony Oliva, Roberto Clemente, Willie Mays, Orlando Cepeda, Whitey Ford, Al Kaline, Willie Stargell, and Sandy Koufax. The fact that the game was played on his home turf made it extra special that Ron Hunt was named as the first Mets player to start an All-Star Game. Hunt went 1-for-3 in the game before being replaced in the batting order by some guy named

Hank Aaron. One year earlier, Hunt finished second in the Rookie of the Year voting to Pete Rose.

Who was the first Mets baserunner to steal home?

Not only did the Mets steal home for the first time as a franchise on this particular play, but they also ended up accomplishing their first-ever triple steal. With the bases loaded in the top of the third inning on September 9, 1963, Dick Smith of the Mets edged off of third base, staring at Philadelphia Phillies pitcher John Boozer. Smith was a seldom-used rookie and not known for his base-stealing prowess. Yet, with his teammate Al Moran at the plate, Smith took off for home and made it safely, sliding in under the late tag of Philadelphia catcher Clay Dalrymple. Following him were Tim Harkness, who stole third base on the play, and Norm Sherry, who stole second, in what was called a "dazzling display of base running." The headline in the *New York Times* captured the state of the Mets and craziness of the moment: "Mets Look Like Major Leaguers with Triple Steal and Two Homers."

When was the first time the Mets left the United States to play? (Hint: They were exhibition games.)

During spring training of 1964, the Mets left their cozy confines of St. Petersburg, Florida, en route for Mexico City for a three-game exhibition series against three Mexican teams. "The expectation of this momentous journey monopolized attention in training camp today," sportswriter Leonard Koppett wrote in the *New York Times*. "The excitement of the impending adventure was in the air." In the first game, Jack Fisher took the mound for the Mets against the Mexico City Red Devils and things did not go well. The Mets made four errors, and could not muster much offense, falling in the exhibition opener, 6–4. The headline in the *New York Times* was a rough one, especially for a friendly international contest: "Same Old Mets Beaten in Mexico." The next night, Tracy Stallard took the hill against the Mexico City Tigers and things went a whole lot better. In that ballgame, the Mets unleashed an offensive barrage to defeat the Tigers, 7–1. Both of those teams were members of the Mexican League, which was part of professional organized baseball with a Double-A classification. In the finale, the Mets took on a combination of the Reds and Tigers, before heading to watch a bullfight.

Who was the first first baseman for the Mets?

The first first baseman for the Mets is one of the most beloved people in the history of the organization. He is a Hall of Famer, yet probably not many Mets fans know he even played for the team, let alone was their first first baseman. However, a glance up high atop left field at Citi Field to the retired numbers section reveals that his #14 is proudly displayed. Yes, legendary Mets manager Gil Hodges, who guided the Miracle Mets to the 1969 world championship, was the team's first-ever first baseman. Hodges, who was a star for the Brooklyn and then Los Angeles Dodgers, returned to play two last seasons with the Mets. In 1962, Hodges appeared in just 54 games for the Mets, but one of those games was the very first, batting fifth—behind Gus Bell and in front of Don Zimmer.

Who was the first player to play for both the Yankees and Mets?

Well, he was certainly not marvelous, but indeed it was Marv Throneberry who earned that distinction when he took the field for the Mets on May 11, 1962. Earlier in his career—in 1955, 1958, and 1959— Throneberry had played for the Yankees. Never a particularly good ballplayer, Throneberry was fantastically bad with the Mets, committing 17 errors in just 97 games in 1962. About a month later, Gene Woodling became the second person to ever play for both the Yankees and Mets when he made his debut for the 1962 Mets. Like many of the Mets from that team, Woodling was just passing through the Polo Grounds on the way to retirement.

Everyone remembers that the legendary Casey Stengel was the first manager of the Mets, but do you know who was the first man to manage the Mets after Casey?

More than midway through the 1965 season, the Mets were wallowing once again at the bottom of the National League. Their 31-64 record did not offer many encouraging signs. Still, Casey Stengel was Casey Stengel and the Mets would never have fired the Ol' Professor. Then, on

July 25, the Mets had a party at the famous Toots Shor's for the players who were invited to attend Old-Timers' Day the next day. While the details remain sketchy, at some point in the evening, Stengel fell off a barstool and broke his hip. Recognizing that considerable rehabilitation would be required at the age of 75, Stengel retired as manager of the Mets on August 30. He was replaced by one of his trusted coaches and 11-year New York Giants veteran catcher, Wes Westrum. The Mets finished the season 19-48 under Westrum, who would manage the team for nearly another two seasons before being fired toward the end of the 1966 campaign. In his time as Mets skipper, Westrum had a record of 142-237.

Who was the Mets' first hitting coach under manager Casey Stengel?

There is a classic saying that states, "Those who can't do, coach." It is often said tongue-in-cheek, but historically it is accurate since most coaches were not the greatest players of their time. In the case of the Mets' first hitting coach, this saying could not be more backward. You see, the Mets first batting coach coached his 1962 Mets lineup to a National League–low batting average of just .240 with a total of 139 homers and 573 RBIs. That same coach, Rogers Hornsby, was one of the most prolific hitters in the history of the game. Over his 23-year career, Hornsby batted a career .358, highlighted by six-straight seasons when he finished the season with batting averages of .370, .397, .401, .384, .424, and .403. Hornsby knew how to hit. However, he put those numbers up from 1920 through 1925. He retired as a player following the 1937 season at the age of 41. That meant that Rogers Hornsby, the batting coach for Casey Stengel and the Mets, was 65 years old. Several months following his one season as the hitting coach for the 1962 Mets, Hornsby suffered a heart attack and died.

Who was the first left-handed pitcher to appear in a game for the Mets?

The Mets did not have a southpaw step on the mound for them until starter Al Jackson made his way to the center of the Polo Grounds diamond in their third game. Despite using a number of pitchers in their first two losses of the 1962 season, the Mets had not used a left-hander out of Casey Stengel's bullpen—not that he had too many options. So it was Al Jackson, who personally suffered 20 of the team's 120 losses that first year, who was the first lefty to pitch for the Mets.

Despite a season marred with tough luck and losses, Jackson's most remarkable outing came at the Polo Grounds on August 14, 1962, when he pitched 15 innings against the Philadelphia Phillies, throwing 215 pitches. He gave up just six hits, but lost when the Phillies rallied thanks to a pair of Mets errors to win 3–1.

Who was the first pitcher to appear in relief for the Mets?

The Mets lost their first-ever game as a franchise by the score of 11–4, so the answer to this question came in that very game. Roger Craig lasted just three innings for the fledgling National League ballclub, allowing five runs on eight hits. In the bottom half of the fourth inning, manager Casey Stengel went to the bullpen for the first time in Mets history and his call went to 24-year-old Bob Moorhead. Unlike Craig, who was in his eighth major-league season, this was Moorhead's first-ever appearance in the majors. It did not go well for the pitcher the Mets drafted from the Cincinnati Reds in the 1961 Rule 5 Draft. Moorhead gave up five runs in his three innings of work. Moorhead went on to appear in 38 games in 1962 for the Mets, but would not have a prolonged career, pitching just a handful of games before retiring following the 1965 season.

Thirteen Mets have hit three home runs in a single game. Who did it first?

Many home-run hitters have accomplished this feat for the Mets. Names like Dave Kingman, Darryl Strawberry, Gary Carter, and Carlos Beltrán are all on the list. However, the man who did it first was Jim Hickman. Not known as one of the game's top sluggers, Hickman had some very impressive power seasons, mostly after his time with the Mets. However, on September 3, 1965, he became the first Mets batter to slug three homers in a single game. The accomplishment came at St. Louis's Sportsman's Park against the Cardinals in a 6–3 Mets victory. Hickman started his big day in the top of the second inning when he blasted a home run deep to center field against Cardinals starter Ray Sadecki that was estimated at 400 feet. Two innings later, Hickman took Sadecki deep again, this time crushing the ball halfway up into the left field bleachers. With the Mets leading by a score of 3–2 in the top of the sixth inning, Hickman got another crack at Sadecki—and once again sent a deep fly well over the left field fence. This homer might have been Hickman's most impressive, as it bounced off a concession stand well beyond the outfield fence. In Hickman's final at-bat, he singled off reliever Nellie Briles, capping off the finest offensive performance of his career, during which he became the all-time home-run leader in franchise history with 53 in his nearly four full seasons with the Mets.

Who drove in the first run ever against the Mets?

This is a significant question only because the answer is such a significant ballplayer from history. Nearing the end of his incredible career, 41-year-old Stan Musial inserted himself into another record book when he drove an RBI-single to left field against Mets starter Roger Craig. The hit scored the speedy Curt Flood, who had led off the game with a single of his own. Musial, who already had 3,539 hits heading into the game, of course, had been a three-time MVP, 24-time All-Star, and had led the National League in batting seven times. It seems unlikely that he considered his RBI against the Mets a career highlight, but it was good enough to be a Mets first.

What was the first official beer of the Mets?

In 1883, New York City was first introduced to Rheingold Beer, which became the main beer consumed in New York State in the 1950s, if you believe the company's claim that it sold 35 percent of the beer in the state. It became the official beer of the New York Mets in 1962, during the Mets' first days in the Polo Grounds, where their huge ad took over almost all of the scoreboard. The H in the Rheingold sign would light up when a hit was credited to a player and the E would light up to signify an error. In a marketing frenzy that combined baseball and women, manager Casey Stengel would appear in many ads with Miss Rheingold—often a model or pretty actress—throughout the 1962 season. Baseball's Ol'

Professor with beverage in hand—now, that was a winning combination. The 1962 Mets, not so much.

Who was the Mets very first baserunning coach?

The first three seasons for the Mets were, let's just say, rough. They had a combined record of 164 wins, 340 losses, and yes, they even had one tie. Good teams tend to be good in most areas. It stands to reason, then, that bad teams—or terrible teams—would do poorly in most areas. In addition to not being able to hit, or pitch, or field very well, the Mets were awful on the bases, as well. They couldn't steal bases, and they were not smart baserunners, for the most part. So, in spring training of 1965 it was time to hire a running coach. This coach would teach them technique and conditioning and ensure that the Mets, whether they possessed speed or not, would be able to improve overall on the basepaths. But the Mets didn't hire just any running coach; they hired perhaps the most famous runner in the nation's history. That's right, in February 1965, Jesse Owens showed up in St. Petersburg to teach the New York Mets how to become better runners, the same Jesse Owens who achieved international fame at the 1936 Summer Olympics in Berlin, winning four gold medals. Oh, and he also was credited with "single-handedly crushing Adolph Hitler's myth of Aryan supremacy," according to author Larry Schwartz. Owens had high hopes for the Mets. "What I want to do," Owens told legendary sportswriter Joseph Durso, "is make the players realize that conditioning is most important in their careers. They all run flat-footed when they come here—it's an occupational thing with baseball players. But now they're up on their toes and they've got some spring when they run." The 51-year-old grandfather of four was convinced that teaching proper technique would make a big difference. "Saving a couple of inches per step can make the difference of a yard or so in the distance between home and first. That can be the difference between an out and a hit—and a run." Unfortunately, the 1965 Mets had fewer hits, scored fewer runs, and won fewer games than the 1964 team. They might have been better off signing Jesse Owens as a pinch-runner.

Who was the first Mets player to appear in an All-Star Game?

Well, this answer is a little convoluted since there were two All Star Games in 1962—just as there had been since 1959 in an effort to make money for the players' pension fund. "It was a slightly daffy idea that sounds nothing but harebrained in retrospect," Richard Sandomir wrote in the *New York Times* in 2008. The first game was played on July 10 at what was known at the time as D.C. Stadium and a second on July 30 at Wrigley Field. So, technically this veteran player, who is the answer to several firsts in Mets history, did not appear in the first game, although he was the Mets' representative. It was not until the game at Wrigley Field that Richie Ashburn, who was an All-Star as a rookie in 1948 for the Philadelphia Phillies, returned to the Midsummer Classic for the final time in a Mets uniform. It was Ashburn's fifth overall selection for the National League and the future Hall of Famer collected a hit in his only at-bat. In 1948, Ashburn was named as an All-Star with his entire brilliant career in front of him. By 1962 he was one of many elder statesmen on the Mets, although he was only 35 years old—but ancient in baseball years. Ashburn batted .306 for the lowly Mets of 1962, but did not officially qualify as a .300 hitter because he did not have enough plate appearances.

Who was the Mets' first overall number one draft pick?

On Tuesday, June 7, 1966, the Mets could have changed their franchise forever. Instead, they drafted catcher Steve Chilcott with the first overall pick of the 1966 Major League Baseball Draft. Chilcott, a high school catcher out of Lancaster, California, is one of only three first overall picks in baseball history to never play a game in the majors. Early on in his minor-league career, Chilcott suffered a variety of injuries and never made it to the Mets. However, that is really only half of the story. The Kansas City Athletics had the second overall pick in the draft, and they selected a guy by the name of Reggie Jackson. Years later, Jackson would say that he was told that the Mets did not draft him because he was dating "out of his race." In his book, *Becoming Mr. October*, Reggie lamented about what could have been. He wrote in his book: "I think about that sometimes. I would've been coming up just as that team was finally improving. They had all those great arms: Tom Seaver, Jerry Koosman, Jon Matlack, Nolan Ryan, Tug McGraw. Oh boy!" For his part, Chilcott's time in baseball was doomed by his bad shoulder. "I just couldn't throw a ball hard enough to break a pane of glass," Chilcott told the *Los Angeles Times* in 1994. "I figured I'd better start finding something else to do." He became a construction supervisor in Santa Barbara. Jackson became a Hall of Famer. "For a while, after I got out of ball, I followed the guys I used to play with," Chilcott said, "and I wondered what would have or could have happened." While the 1965 draft was the first in MLB history, that year the Mets had the number two pick despite having the worst record in 1964. That is because it was determined that teams would pick in reverse order of winning records, but that they would alternate between leagues, with the American League selecting first. Kansas City ended up picking Rick Monday with that very first pick.

Who pitched the first no-hitter against the Mets?

Everyone remembers, or at least many remember, when Philadelphia's Jim Bunning threw a perfect game against the Mets on Father's Day at Shea Stadium in 1964. However, Bunning was not the first pitcher to throw a no-hitter against the Mets. You are probably guessing that the 1962 team must figure into this answer somehow and indeed you would be correct. It was New York on New York crime—well, not really—but it might have felt that way when Brooklyn's own took the mound for Brooklyn's own Los Angeles Dodgers on June 30, 1962. This was one year before Koufax truly became Koufax, and turned out to be the first of what would be four career no-hitters for the lefty. Koufax struck out 13 Mets and walked three en route to a 5–0 victory. An interesting postscript to this no-hitter is that until 2007, no one had realized that the legendary Vin Scully's call of the game had been recorded. "This was so unheard of, when we first thought that it could exist, there's just no way that there's a recording of this because it would have surfaced after all these years," Dodgers historian Mark Langill told National Public Radio. But it did exist and it did surface in 2007, allowing us to hear in Scully's melodic tones what the scene was like that day in Los Angeles. "All of the Dodgers are out to mob Koufax, halfway between third and home," Scully proclaimed. "He is the first Dodgers left-hander to pitch a no-hitter since way back in 1908, and he is now walking toward home plate and the crowd is giving him a standing ovation."

STADIUM FIRSTS

FOR A YOUNG BASEBALL FAN, OR ANY BASEBALL FAN FOR THAT MATTER, their team's home stadium is much more than just a ballpark—it is a second home. It doesn't matter how new, or how run-down that stadium is, for a baseball fan, it is the place where their team plays—case closed. Having started my journey as a baseball fan in the mid-1970s, in the rotting, smelly, dirty, cavernous, and often empty Shea Stadium, I know of what I speak. The facts are these: I smelled the smells, felt the dirt under my feet and seat, and walked up and down miles and miles of concrete ramps—and loved every second of it. You know why? The Mets played in that stadium. Long before the phrase, "It's a dump, but it's our dump," was coined, the sentiment was there. It was where the Mets played, and to be able to go there was an honor and a privilege. As you get older, you realize that Shea was not without its failings—smell and dirt aside. You could walk around the entire interior stadium and never see the field. It was entirely possible that you had a seat in the field level that faced directly into short center field, which meant you had to rotate your entire body to the left or right in order to see the batter. Still, it was Shea—not the Mets' first ballpark, but certainly their most iconic—to date.

In the winter of 2008, Citi Field was nearly complete and would certainly be ready in time for Opening Day in 2009. The Mets had played their final game at Shea months earlier and the demolition of the big stadium was well underway. While taking a tour of the new ballpark, fate would bring me to a staircase down the left field line. By now, it is a set of steps that I have taken hundreds of times. However, this was my first trip up—and it was the one I will remember forever. After reaching the first landing, the sight straight ahead of us was beautiful and hideous—Shea

Stadium was literally being torn down before our eyes. Heavy machinery, dump trucks, and piles of debris stood where I remember watching Doc Gooden pitch, and Mike Piazza hit, and David Wright field. The hulking scoreboard was gone and the only pieces remaining were the mezzanine and upper deck sections. As we stood there, giant chunks of the stadium I spent so many fun afternoons and nights in fell to the ground as if it were just any other building being torn down. It was hard to come to terms with how the Shea of my past would blend with this day and my last view of Shea. However, change is good—and I happened to be standing on a staircase within the brand-new ballpark that the Mets would be playing in. It wouldn't just be Citi Field—it would be where the Mets play. That will always be enough.

Let's take a walk back through some of the many firsts in the history of the Mets' three stadiums. Please note that there will be no postseason stadium questions in this chapter, as those will come later in the book.

What was the first stadium that the Mets called home?

This might seem like an easy one to start off with, but there might be some legit, hard-core Mets fans who don't know that the Polo Grounds was the first stadium of the Mets. However, it was the fourth rendition of the Polo Grounds. In a confusing history that has been the subject of books on its own, the easiest way to explain it is that the Mets played in the final version of Polo Grounds IV, which was once known as Brotherhood Park. The poor conditions of the stadium in upper Manhattan played a big role in the New York Giants' move to San Francisco following the 1957 season. With no tenants, the Polo Grounds just sat—and sat—practically abandoned. Then, after sitting vacant for nearly three years, the Titans of New York, today known as the New York Jets, began to play there in 1960. The Polo Grounds was still usable, and it was decided that the Mets would play there as well as an interim home while Shea Stadium was being built. The Mets indeed played in the very stadium that Willie Mays had made his legendary catch in center field and where Bobby Thomson hit his "Shot Heard 'Round the World." During the Mets' time there, there were no such memorable occasions. Although New York City did spend nearly $350,000 to update the cavernous old building, which included installation of a new field, updated lighting, and painting the ballpark in Mets' colors of blue and orange. Some actually referred to the aesthetic changes to the stadium as applying makeup to a corpse. Following the 1963 season, Shea Stadium would be ready for the Mets in the borough of Queens, across the river at the World's Fair Grounds. The Polo Grounds was mercifully demolished in 1964 using the same wrecking ball that had taken down Ebbets Field in Brooklyn four years earlier. The site is now home to a public housing project opened in 1968 and managed by the New York City Housing Authority.

What was really the first stadium that the Mets called home?

Wait, didn't we just deal with that in the previous question? Yes, you were going to confidently say the Polo Grounds and you would

The Polo Grounds was the first home of the Mets, serving the team in 1962 and 1963. In their games played at the Polo Grounds, the Mets had 56 wins and 105 losses.

THE SPORTING NEWS ARCHIVES, PUBLIC DOMAIN, VIA WIKIMEDIA COMMONS

be—technically incorrect. What? Why did you just waste the past five minutes reading the last question and answer if it was not true? Well, it was true—and it wasn't. Just under 1,200 miles south of the site of the Polo Grounds in St. Petersburg, Florida, is Al Lang Field—the spring training home of the New York Mets from 1962 through 1987. The Mets shared the facility with the St. Louis Cardinals, who historically had at times shared Al Lang Field with both the New York Yankees and the New York Giants. The Mets played their first-ever official spring training game on Saturday, March 10, 1962, dropping a decision to their room-mates, the Cardinals. Losing would not be a rarity in 1962 for the Mets. In 2011, after 60-plus years of being home to various baseball teams, Al Lang Stadium was reconfigured to better host soccer and is the current residence of the Tampa Bay Rowdies.

Who was the Mets' first head groundskeeper at the Polo Grounds?

Many people remember the great Pete Flynn as the head groundskeeper for many years at Shea Stadium. Flynn, however, who was with the Mets since the beginning, actually was not the first man to tend to the Mets field—first at the Polo Grounds and then Shea Stadium. That was the man who hired Flynn, the great John McCarthy—himself a legendary groundskeeper. McCarthy had worked as a groundskeeper for the Yankees at Yankee Stadium in the 1950s, long before becoming the Mets' top man in 1962. However, it was in 1969 when the Mets clinched the National League East at Shea Stadium that McCarthy went from head groundskeeper to savior! Following the final out of the division-clinching game, fans stormed the field and ripped it to shreds—leaving a lot of dirt and some grassy clumps. Intent to make sure the Mets would have a playable field for the first-ever National League Championship Series, and eventually the World Series, he and his team did more than make it playable: They made it almost as good as new. He turned the head groundskeeper reins over to Flynn and worked in the Mets front office until his death in 1994.

What was the price for a field box seat at the very first Mets game at the Polo Grounds?

Friday, April 13, 1962: New York Mets, game number one. There was not even an opponent's name on the ticket (there actually wouldn't be in the Mets' two seasons at the Polo Grounds). However, there was a price—for pretty much any box seat in the stadium, it would set you back $3.50 per ticket. By normal inflation, that would come out to approximately $35 in 2023 monies. Something has gone wrong, somewhere. The actual price of a field box seat at Citi Field—sold by the Mets—in 2023, started at around $100 and ended in the thousands, depending on the game and the exact seat location. Parking at Citi Field in 2023 was $40 per car. While the Polo Grounds did have some parking, it was not much, mostly because the stadium's final incarnation had opened just two years after Ford's Model T was introduced. The price of that Model T was $825.

Who was the first Mets pitcher to earn a win at the Polo Grounds?

Earlier in the book, we learned that Jay Hook was the pitcher who won the first-ever game for the Mets. However, that was on the road—in Pittsburgh. The Mets did not win their first home game until the 14th game of the season. After Hook's road victory against the Pirates, the Mets lost three straight games to fall to 1-12 on the season. On April 28, 1962, in front of just over 10,000 fans at the Polo Grounds, it was Hook again who went to the mound as the starter. However, this would not be Hook's night to make it once again to the record books. Instead, the only Mets pitcher to have a win to date went only two-thirds of an inning against the Philadelphia Phillies, and gave up four runs on four hits, including two home runs. On this night, however, Philadelphia pitchers were not up to the task either and the Mets rallied to take the lead. For the final three innings, manager Casey Stengel turned to starting pitcher Roger Craig to take over, which he did. In Craig's three innings he gave up just one hit to secure the first home victory for the Mets. The next day, the Mets defeated the Phillies in game one of a doubleheader for the team's first-ever winning streak. It was short-lived, however, as the Phils took game two by the score of 10–2.

Who was the first concessions company for the Mets?

At the turn of the century—the 20th century—no man was more influential in the world of stadiums than Harry M. Stevens, who emigrated to the United States in the late 1880s, fell in love with the sport of baseball, and created a concessions company in New Jersey. The man, who would eventually become known as a concessionaire extraordinaire, invented the modern scorecard, brought the hot dog to the Polo Grounds, and was a part of the New York landscape from 1900 through the mid-1990s. That is when Harry M. Stevens Inc. was acquired by the concessions conglomerate Aramark, which still services many ballparks throughout the nation, including Citi Field and Yankee Stadium.

Who was the first-ever public address announcer for the Mets?

This took some real digging and if you happen to get it, bravo! Actually, the Mets first PA announcer at the Polo Grounds was better known for his calls of harness racing in the New York area, specifically at the now defunct Roosevelt Raceway on Long Island. However, in 1962, Jack E. Lee was named the voice of the Polo Grounds for the Mets. He moved with the Mets to Shea Stadium and held the position until the end of the 1966 season. In addition to his horse racing and baseball work, he was the ring announcer at Madison Square Garden for the WWF for a time in the 1970s.

Which Mets player hit the first home run at the Polo Grounds?

For those who remember the 1962 Mets, this answer makes perfect sense. For those who do not remember the 1962 Mets, Frank Thomas is a guy whose name you should know. Thomas, who hit the first-ever long ball for the Mets in the very first game the team played there, led the team in 1962 with 34 home runs. His first of the year came in the Mets' 4–3 loss to the Pirates in the Mets' inaugural Opening Day at the Polo Grounds off of Pittsburgh starting pitcher Tom Sturdivant. In fact, the Mets had acquired Thomas from the Milwaukee Braves in November 1961 for his penchant to hit home runs. From 1953 through 1961—playing for the Pirates, Reds, Cubs, and Braves—Thomas had hit exactly 200 home runs, an average of 22 per season. So his 35 homers in

1962 were certainly a welcome sight for a team which only hit 139 home runs in all. Thomas was responsible for 25 percent of the Mets' home runs in that fateful first season. His 94 runs batted in also led the team by a country mile. Thomas passed away in January 2023 at the age of 93.

Who was the first Met pitcher to record a win at Shea Stadium?

In Terry Cashman's New York Mets version of his song "Talkin' Baseball," there was a lyric, "Al Jackson, he always did his best." That was very true, although to paraphrase another song, often Jackson's best was not good enough. After compiling a 21-37 record with the lowly 1962 and 1963 Mets, Jackson deserved a little piece of the Mets' record book. In 1964, the Mets opened the season with two games in Philadelphia. Jackson pitched—and lost—the opener. Five days later, the 0-4 Mets hosted the Pittsburgh Pirates for the finale of a three-game series. This time, Jackson made it into the record books. Luckily, this would be a record that would last forever, as you can never have another first—as illustrated often throughout this book. So when Jackson completely shut down the Pirates over nine innings, yielding just six hits, Jackson earned the first-ever victory for the Mets at Shea, as well as the first-ever shutout at Shea. That day, without a doubt, Al Jackson certainly did his best.

Who was the first member of the Mets to hit a home run into the upper deck of Shea Stadium?

This is one of those first and only answers, because only one man in history ever hit a fair ball into the upper deck at Shea. That honor goes to Mets center fielder Tommie Agee, who launched a low pitch from Montreal's Larry Jaster in the second inning on April 10, 1969, an estimated 505 feet into the left field seats. The Mets commemorated the amazin' feat by painting a plaque onto the wall where the ball hit. The plaque was painted onto the actual cement wall of Shea Stadium and remained there for three decades. Before Shea was demolished following the 2008 season, the plaque was thankfully removed and sold to a private collector, who reportedly has it on display in his backyard.

Tommie Agee was the first and only player to hit a home run into the upper deck at Shea Stadium.
BERNARD GOTFRYD, PUBLIC DOMAIN, VIA WIKIMEDIA COMMONS

Before being known as Shea Stadium, what was the first name of the big stadium in Flushing?

Officially, the giant horseshoe on the edge of the World's Fair Grounds in Flushing Meadows Park was always known as Shea Stadium, named in honor of William Shea—a New York lawyer who had been integral to the process of bringing National League baseball back to New York. However, initially the stadium had unofficially been known as Flushing Meadows Municipal Stadium. New York bigwigs always had an alternate name for the field, however. "You can't do that," Shea was saying to New York City mayor Robert Wagner on the other end of the line. "Come up with something else." Shea had become increasingly embarrassed by the thought of having the giant, multipurpose stadium named in his honor. "We're going to do it," Mayor Wagner told him. Shea tried to reach Wagner's office before the announcement had been made, but to no avail. He was too late—he had himself a stadium. William A. Shea Municipal Stadium, eventually just Shea Stadium. Perhaps Shea was not embarrassed about the name itself, but by the fact that the "glistening new state-of-the-art ballpark, was awash in human waste," according to the *New York Daily News.* Under the stands, raw sewage floated through its tunnels, drifting into the clubhouses, seeping into the carpets. From Day One, Shea Stadium was built like a brick outhouse. "We were pushing it off, trying to keep it off the field," says legendary groundskeeper Pete Flynn, who was an assistant at the time. "It was a nightmare." The pumps in the boiler room had failed and the foul-smelling filth of 50,312 fans flooded the building. "It was not a good way to start off Opening Day," remembered Flynn. Long after the sewage was ever cleaned up . . . wait, was it ever cleaned up? In any event, Shea was once quoted as saying, "They'll probably change the name 15 minutes after I am dead." That never happened. Shea passed away in 1991. Today the pedestrian bridge in right-center field at Citi Field bears Shea's name.

Who threw out the very first ceremonial first pitch in the history of Shea Stadium?

Well, he protested, he protested, and then he took to the mound on April 17, 1964. Before Jack Fisher of the Mets had the opportunity to throw his first pitch against the Pittsburgh Pirates, William Shea himself made his way to the mound in front of what would eventually be 50,312 excited fans. Of course, when Shea arrived on the mound the stadium was not nearly full to capacity due to the traffic jam at and around the sparkling new stadium that bore his name. "The lack of parking space at the stadium caused massive traffic snarls that started an hour and a half before game time," sportswriter Leonard Koppett wrote on page one of the *New York Times.* "In every respect but traffic control and the outcome of the game, the occasion was declared a rousing success by most of those involved." One of the most striking aspects of the day was the attendance, with more than 50,000 fans packed into the new stadium. One day earlier in the Bronx, just over 12,700 fans showed up for Opening Day at Yankee Stadium, despite the Yankees having won the American League pennant the previous year—perhaps a sign that the fans thought their loss to the Dodgers in the 1963 World Series meant the Bronx Bombers' glory days might be behind them. Koppett wrote, "Now, a team that had finished a most decided last in both years of its existence, pulled in almost four times as many people with no promise whatever of finishing anything but last again." Forty-four years later, Bill Shea Jr., the son of William Shea, threw out the first pitch of the final Opening Day in the history of the stadium named for his dad.

Who was the first Mets batter to step up to the plate at Shea Stadium?

Throughout the pages of this book, you have no doubt read—and will read—about players who played for the Mets whose names you just don't remember. Then, there are some you had just never heard of in the first place. This answer might very well fall into that category, as even the truest fan of the Orange and Blue might be unable to get this. You can try to solve this one by using deduction. For one thing, it had to be in 1964—the first year that Shea was open—which means you have to know the 1964 Mets roster pretty well. By their third season of play, aging veterans such as Gil Hodges, Richie Ashburn, and Duke Snider had either moved on or retired. The 1964 roster had a few familiar names, like Ed Kranepool and Ron Hunt, but many more no-name names, as it were. In the first game of the season in Philadelphia, the Mets leadoff hitter was first baseman Dick Smith and in the second game of the season—also at Connie Mack Stadium, Kranepool had the honors. However, in the third game of the season—the home opener at Shea—the Mets used a third different leadoff hitter in as many games, which would—obviously—serve as the answer to this question. That would be—first baseman Tim Harkness. Told you! Harkness had been with the Mets in 1963 after two seasons in Los Angeles with the Dodgers. He was traded in November 1962 for another, not-so-legendary Mets player, Bob Miller, who went 1-12 as a pitcher for New York in 1962. Harkness appeared in 123 games for the Mets in 1963, but only managed a batting average of .211. However, 1964 was not a time of many options for manager Casey Stengel, who tapped Harkness to lead off the game and the home season against Pittsburgh Pirates starter Bob Friend. The result was a groundball to shortstop for the Mets' first-ever out at Shea Stadium.

What was the first season that the Mets had the ability to show photographs of the players on their scoreboard at Shea Stadium?

It depends on whether you attended a day or night game at Shea in its debut season. The 60-ton, state of the art scoreboard from the very first day had the ability to show color slides of players. As per the 1963 Mets yearbook, "At the top of the scoreboard an eighteen by twenty-four foot rear-projection screen will permit the display of full-color photographs of each player as he takes his turn at bat. Color motion pictures may also be shown to the entire stadium audience through the 'Photorama' screen." Well ahead of its time, it would be another two decades before most stadiums had videos projected from the stadium scoreboard. In fact, almost no other stadium scoreboard even had the ability to show color slides. The only problem was that the screen at Shea was, let's just say, less than perfect. In fact it almost never worked. Due to the rear-projection technology at the time, the photo was impossible to see during day games. By midway through the 1964 season, the projector was covered with a giant Mets logo. There is no record of it ever showing color motion pictures, despite the high praise from the *New York Times* prior to the stadium opening. "Movies in color can also be shown, should the need arise, for example, while waiting out a rain squall." One interesting side note about the Shea scoreboard is that when the New York Yankees played at Shea Stadium during the 1974 and 1975 seasons, there was no way for the scoreboard to denote DH in the lineup area. There was no designated hitter when the scoreboard was built in 1964, and there was no DH in the National League at the time. Instead, the lineup displayed a "B" next to the batter who was serving as the DH to signify "batter."

When did the Mets debut their famous large-capped bullpen cart?

The Mets introduced their bullpen cart—a golf cart with an oversized team hat and two bats as the front poles—at the start of the 1967 season. Several years earlier, the Los Angeles Angels used a plain old, regular golf cart to bring in relief pitchers, but there was no pizazz at all.

The Mets' version was an electric Pullman chassis, along with the giant cap, which drove starting pitchers out to begin the game, then brought in relief pitchers from the bullpen. Eventually, the visiting team would get their own cart, as well, and the Mets had giant hats for each of the National League teams. By most accounts, the Mets were the first team to have bullpen carts such as these. Even the Hall of Fame lacks documentation—a tiny moment in baseball history that has totally been lost to time. What has not been lost in time is one of the Mets' original carts, which was sold as part of a New York–themed auction by Sotheby's in 2015 for $112,500.

Who hit the first inside-the-park home run at Shea Stadium?

This little nugget is lost, buried really, within a 16–3 loss to the Los Angeles Dodgers in the first game of a Sunday afternoon doubleheader on June 5, 1966. However, in the inconsequential bottom of the eighth inning of that contest, Ron Hunt hit a very consequential flyball to center field that bounded off of the wall. Hunt sped around the bases. As the ball bounded away from Dodger center fielder Wes Parker, who had relocated from first base earlier in the game, the first-ever Mets All-Star representative two seasons earlier circled the bases into the history books.

What was the first-ever concert held at Shea Stadium? What song did the band open up with?

Ahh, the dreaded two-part nonbaseball question. Still, it is relevant given how important Shea Stadium was, not just to Mets fans, but to fans of music throughout the years. From the Police, to Eric Clapton, to the Rolling Stones, Springsteen, Billy Joel—so many played at Shea. Of course, no concert was as well known and memorable as the first, which took place August 15, 1965. That is when four lads from Liverpool made their way across the pond to tour America. Not only was that night memorable because it was the first stop on the Beatles summer tour in 1965, and not only was it the first concert in the history of Shea Stadium, but it was also the first-ever open-air stadium rock concert. The Beatles, who performed on a makeshift stage near where second base would normally be, earned a whopping $160,000 for their 30-minute set—which was a record payout at that time. In the book, *Beatles Anthology*, Ringo Starr remembered the show: "What I remember most about the concert was that we were so far away from the audience. . . . And screaming had become the thing to do. . . . Everybody screamed. If you look at the footage, you can see how we reacted to the place. It was very big and very strange." As to the second part of the question—what song did the band open up with—appropriately, the Beatles started the evening with "Twist and Shout." In all, the Beatles played 12 hits that night. When the Mets returned to Shea following the concert, it took them three games to compile 12 hits!

Who was the first pianist who tickled the ivories of the Shea Stadium organ from 1964 to 1978?

This one you either know, or you don't; there is really no in between. In 1964, the Mets acquired organist Jane Jarvis from the Milwaukee Braves for a musician to be named later. Well, sort of. After eight years playing for the Braves at County Stadium in Milwaukee, Jarvis—a well-known jazz pianist and composer—moved to New York City and became a fixture at Shea Stadium, performing a repertoire that mixed jazz staples like Charlie Parker's "Scrapple from the Apple" with more conventional fare like "Take Me Out to the Ballgame" and "Meet the Mets." According to writer Lee Lowenfish, when Mets general manager George Weiss was asked about Jarvis, he said, "We want to give the fans good music if we can't give them good baseball." One of Jarvis's most memorable performances was May 31, 1964, during a doubleheader against the San Francisco Giants. The two games combined for nearly 10 hours, and when it was all over, Jarvis played "Gee, How I Hate to Get Up in the Morning." In 1979, Jarvis left the Mets and baseball entirely to concentrate on her first musical love, jazz piano. She became a fixture at New York nightclubs from her mid-60s into her 90s. But for more than two decades she was best known as a ballpark organist.

When was the first time the Mets drew more than two million fans in a single season?

Inexplicably, the 1966 Mets—who finished ninth in the National League and lost 95 games—finished second in the league attendance standings. However, that 1966 team—still one season away from the debut of a young kid named Tom Seaver—fell just short of the two million mark, finishing with 1,932,693 fans crossing through the turnstiles at Shea Stadium. It was not until the amazing year of 1969 that 2,175,373 fans came to see the Mets play at Shea, leading the National League in attendance. In fact, the Mets would lead the NL in most home fans in 1969, 1970, 1971, and 1972, drawing more than two million people in each of those seasons. Those seasons, at least, the Mets had developed some pedigree, had won a world championship, and headed toward another National League pennant. In 1966, though, the Mets fans were still just an optimistic group, showing up to cheer their team on night after night.

When was the first time the Mets drew more than three million fans in a single season?

At first thought, this would appear to be an easy question to answer. It has to be one of their championship seasons and it has to be at Shea Stadium. That leaves 1969, 1973, or 1986. However, none of those answers would be correct. In 1969, as the Mets were winning 100 games for the first time in franchise history, en route to stunning the world and winning the World Series, the Mets drew 2,175,373 fans. That was an average attendance of 26,529 fans per game—less than half of Shea's capacity. Still, that was still good enough to lead the entire National League in attendance. The following season, in 1970, the team drew more than 2.6 million fans—hint, hint! We can discount the 1973 National League champions, because despite reaching the World Series in October, the regular season had many ups and down and the Mets fell short of even two million fans that season. That leaves 1986, the Mets' best regular season ever—with 108 victories, All-Stars galore—and an unbelievable energy at Shea Stadium nearly every night. However, remember the hint from above: the year following a championship season has always meant more at the turnstiles than the actual winning season. In 1986, the Mets averaged 34,168 fans per home game, giving them a total of 2,767,601 fans for the year. It was not until the following season, in 1987, that the Mets finally broke the three million mark! That season, the Orange and Blue drew a total of 3,034,129 fans to Shea, an average of 37,458 per game. Throughout their history, the Mets broke the three-million mark in attendance six times—topping four million fans once, as discussed elsewhere in this book.

What was the first year that the Mets Home Run Apple made its home beyond the center field fence at Shea Stadium?

As the Mets entered the 1980s, fresh off of one of the worst years in the history of the franchise, ownership was looking for something to entice fans to come to the ballpark. In 1979, a year that the Mets did nothing but lose—without the lovableness of the early 1960s Mets—only 788,905 fans came out to Shea. That's an average of 9,740 per game in a stadium that held more than 55,000. So, the Mets decided to put a giant, nine-foot-tall, 582-pound hunk of fiberboard and wire in the shape of an apple—you know, because New York was the Big Apple—and raise it out of a 10-foot-tall black plywood top hat each time the Mets hit a home run. It was supposed to be like a magician's hat, and on the front of the hat, in a bold script font, it read "Mets Magic." That went hand-in-hand with the team's slogan that year, "The Magic Is Back." Only it wasn't. The Mets only won 67 games in 1980, and the Home Run Apple very often would get stuck on the way up or down. However, the apple caught on, and more than 90 percent of fans voted that they wanted to have a similar apple in the new ballpark when the Mets left Shea and moved next door to Citi Field. Today's apple dwarfs the original—which sits outside the main rotunda of Citi Field. The new apple measures 16½ feet tall and is 18 feet in diameter. The outer shell of the apple weighs 4,800 pounds, and its hidden cantilevered frame, which is powered by the hydraulic setup that lifts the apple, weighs 9,000 pounds.

Who was the starting pitcher for the Mets for the first-ever game at Shea Stadium?

There were a lot of Mets firsts on just this one question, as it turns out. It was the first Opening Day ever at Shea Stadium and the stadium was hardly ready for prime time. Just hours before the crowd of 50,000-plus fans were scheduled to start filing through the turnstiles for the first time, head groundskeeper John McCarthy and his crew were dealing with several on-field hindrances, such as drainage problems in the outfield.

In addition, the outfield fence was not finished being painted, and there were, reportedly, sewage issues in some of the restrooms. Still, in the first game he ever pitched for the Mets, Jack Fisher climbed to the top of the brand-new mound at Shea Stadium that afternoon to face the Pittsburgh Pirates. Fisher pitched into the seventh inning for the Mets, giving up three earned runs on 11 hits, taking the loss. In the contest, Fisher gave up the first-ever home run to an opposing player at Shea when future Hall of Famer Willie Stargell blasted one over the semi-painted fence.

This question truly only works in a multiple-choice format. Which of these are true? Shea Stadium was the first stadium of its kind to:

1. **Have an extensive escalator system**

2. **Have an electronic scoreboard**

3. **Have almost no light towers**

4. **Have every seat directed at the center of the field**

5. **All of the above**

6. **None of the above**

Almost always, if there is a multiple choice question that offers an "all of the above" option, I would say go that direction. It applies here, as well. All four of those things listed were true of Shea Stadium, which was considered to be a state-of-the-art multipurpose stadium when it opened in 1964. (1) For those who remember the stadium well, those tremendously steep escalators, some as long as 120 feet. In all, Shea had 21 escalators, which were designed to move as many as 56,000 individuals an hour, according to the Mets' 1964 yearbook. Those escalators, along with the iconic ramps on the outer perimeter of the stadium, made Shea a particularly memorable place to get in and out of. (2) That tremendous Shea scoreboard in right-center field stood 86 feet high, 175 feet wide, and weighed over 60 tons. The original scoreboard included 28,000 lights and 80 miles of cable wiring, and rarely worked well in its earliest days.

Rheingold Beer, the original official beer of the Mets, financed the cost of the scoreboard. While it is true that the 1962 version of the Polo Grounds did have some sort of smaller electronic scoreboard rigged up for the Mets, Shea is considered to be the first of its kind. (3) From the day that they first turned on the lights at Shea Stadium, it was the "brightest ballpark in the majors." Speaking in layman's terms, Lou Bean, the chief electrician, explained that the 820 incandescent quartz lights, which go on immediately, "blend" the 884 mercury vapor lights into a pure white. Sure, makes perfect sense. The biggest improvement over other stadiums was that Shea had only two small light towers, located in the outfield. Most of the lights were on top of the "curving necklace that rings the top of the stands, except for a stretch in the middle. This is so that outfielders won't have to look up into the glare," said the *New York Times*. The players were overjoyed by the lighting at their new home. "There are no shadows at all," Mets shortstop Al Moran said in the *New York Times*. "It's so clear, you can see an ant crawling on the grass." (4) Shea was the first ballpark in which every seat in the permanently fixed stands was directed at the center of the field. As an added bonus, there was not a single column or stanchion that obstructed the fan's view of the action. The firm of architects and engineers that designed Shea Stadium was Praeger-Kavanagh-Waterbury of New York City. Because it was built for both baseball and football, the seats were very far from the playing field. However, as a baseball fan, facing the center of the field was awful. You had to turn, almost completely, to see what was happening at home plate.

From the 1980s through the day it was torn down, Shea Stadium was known for its orange field-level seats, blue loge-level seats, green mezzanine-level seats, and red upper deck seats. However, what colors were these sections when the ballpark first opened in 1964?

There seemed to be no rhyme or reason to how the builders of Shea Stadium selected its seat colors. Often, a stadium will reflect the color of its home team. The Mets have never really subscribed to that in their history, as even now at Citi Field the seats are dark green—a color that has never been associated with the Mets at all. When Shea opened in

Shea Stadium was the site of so many Mets firsts! In fact, it was a first of its own—
as it was the first true home of the Mets. For the franchise's first two seasons, the
Mets played at the Polo Grounds, former home of the New York (baseball) Giants,
New York Yankees, New York (football) Giants, and many other teams.
YIFTACHSAM, PUBLIC DOMAIN, VIA WIKIMEDIA COMMONS

1964, as part of the World's Fair in Flushing Meadows Park, each of the
four levels had wooden seats with very distinct colors—not unlike most
big ballparks built in the 1960s and 1970s. At Shea, if you were seated
in the field-level seats, you would—for some reason—be in yellow seats.
These seats often looked to be more like white in the bright sunlight and
as the years went by. The loge-level seats were brownish, the mezzanine
was blue, and the upper deck was greenish. Two interesting notes: The
box seats in each section were slightly darker than the reserved seats in
each section, and the game tickets matched the color of the section that
you were sitting in. That all changed during the 1980 season when all of
the wooden seats were replaced by plastic seats in the more recent color
scheme.

Who was the first—and only—non-Mets player to cause the Home Run Apple at Shea Stadium to rise?

Well, he wasn't a member of the Mets at that point of his career, but Darryl Strawberry had caused that oversized Home Run Apple in right-center field to rise out of its top hat many times from 1983 through 1990. In fact, of the 252 regular-season home runs that Strawberry stroked for the Mets throughout his eight-year Mets career, a record 123 of those were hit at Shea Stadium. You see, since the apple was installed beyond the outfield fence at Shea during the 1980 season, each time a member of the Mets hit a home run over the fence, the nine-foot-tall, 600-pound apple—featuring the Mets logo on its belly—would come to life and rise out of the top hat. In the early days, the fruit of the day had many technical issues and often needed to be repaired throughout the season. When the apple was first installed, the inscription in front read: "Mets Magic"—thus the pulling a rabbit out of a hat motif. A few years later, as there was little magic at Shea in the early 1980s, the inscription was changed to "HOME RUN." It had never, however, gone up for a non-Mets home run—until April 1998, when the New York Yankees were forced to borrow Shea when a 500-pound beam fell in the stands at Yankee Stadium, closing it for a few days. Strawberry, who was now playing his fourth season as a member of the Yankees, launched a familiar sight of the 1980s, homering off Omar Olivares in the bottom of the fifth inning. Someone up in the Shea Stadium press box then decided to have a little fun and hit the button that sent the apple out of its hat. It traveled up a few feet, before retreating back into the hat before the Mets' logo could be revealed. Still, a moment that has lived on. "That definitely was a good memory," Strawberry told reporters after the game, "because I've seen it a lot of times."

What team did the Mets host at Shea in the opponent's first-ever and last-ever game?

Since part of this question asks the reader to name the "last-ever" game for this team, then clearly this team is no longer around. That narrows it down considerably since only one team came into the National League after the Mets and has now ceased to exist. Yes, it is the Montreal

Expos. On April 8, 1969, the Expos traveled to Queens to play in their very first major-league game and defeated the Mets by a score of 11–10. The Expos offense was led by Maury Wills, Rusty Staub, and the ever-memorable Coco Laboy. Tom Seaver was roughed up by Montreal, but only allowed two earned runs and did not get the loss against his record; that went to Cal Koonce. For the Mets, Tommie Agee and Duffy Dyer each drove in three runs in the loss. Then, just 35 years later, on October 3, 2004, the Mets defeated the Expos in their final game, 8–1. In the victory, David Wright went 2-for-3, with a home run and three RBIs. Starter Tom Glavine got the win, while Montreal's John Patterson endured the final loss. The following season, the Montreal Expos would become the Washington Nationals.

Who was the first Mets batter to step into the batter's box at Citi Field for a regular-season game?

The first visiting batter at Citi Field in its inaugural 2009 season was the same player who hit the first home run in Citi Field history. Both of those honors go to Jody Gerut of the San Diego Padres, who homered off of Mike Pelfrey to christen the stadium. Not exactly the way the Mets drew it up. However, about 15 minutes later, the Mets finally came to bat and their leadoff hitter—José Reyes—stepped into the batter's box for the very first time in the new digs. Batting against Walter Silva, Reyes hit a groundball to first baseman Adrián González, who handled it himself and stepped on the bag to retire Reyes. Reyes would play the 2009, 2010, and 2011 seasons for the Mets, winning the National League batting title in 2011. On this Monday night, however, the scorecard simply read "3 unassisted" after one batter for the Mets.

Which Mets pitcher recorded the first-ever win for the Mets at Citi Field?

Some questions have obvious answers and some simply do not. Unless you specifically remember the first game that the Mets won at home in 2009 at their new stadium, this one might need an educated guess. To make things even more complicated, the Mets played their first six games of the 2009 season on the road, starting the season in

Cincinnati and then Miami, before returning home to face the San Diego Padres on April 13. The Mets lost that first game at Citi Field to the Padres by the score of 6–5. So it was not until April 14, in the Mets' eighth game of the season, that Oliver Pérez went to the mound as the Mets' starting pitcher to lead the team to victory. Pérez had lost his first start of the season, but on this night he was sharp. The southpaw went six innings, gave up just one run on three hits, and the Mets offense provided more than enough punch, going on to win the contest 7–2 in front of 35,581 fans at Citi Field. The rest of the 2009 season was not as kind to Oliver Pérez, as the 27-year-old would win just two more games. However, Pérez would endure—pitching through the 2022 season.

What was the first Major League Baseball team—other than the Mets—to call Citi Field home for a game?

Over the years, the Yankees had "borrowed" Shea Stadium from the Mets multiple times, sometimes for a single game, and once for two full seasons. However, in 2017 it was the Tampa Bay Rays that occupied the home dugout and clubhouse at Citi Field against the Yankees. This time, however, it had nothing to do with the Yankees. The three-game series that was scheduled to be played at Tropicana Field in St. Petersburg, Florida, had to be moved to Citi Field in New York due to Hurricane Irma. "After much consideration, our games against the Yankees will be moved to Citi Field as Hurricane Irma approaches Florida," Rays president Brian Auld noted in his press release. "We are grateful to the Mets for opening their doors to us. We are most concerned with the safety of our fans, our families, friends and neighbors." Since the decision was made just days before the game, the seats to the upper two levels weren't sold, and were blocked off to the fans. The lower levels were filled as much as they would be if the game were in the Bronx; however in Queens—on this night—the seats only cost $25 apiece. Even without any bleachers, there was a roll call for the Yankees fielders and "Let's go Yankees" chants. Manager Joe Girardi even admitted it felt like a home game. Evan Longoria, one of the Tampa Bay stars in 2017, tweeted: "We're @ CitiField and I get the honor of having Mr. Met, David Wright's locker. Thanks to all the @Mets staff who have been so accommodating." The

Yankees won the game, 5–1, and took the three-game series, two games to one.

Who hit the first home run in the history of Citi Field?

Hint—it happened so quickly in the very first game at Citi Field, that the answer to this question could not possibly be a Met. The answer to who gave up the first home run at Citi Field, however, is a Met and that player's name is Mike Pelfrey. Starting against the San Diego Padres in the opener, Pelfrey faced leadoff hitter Jody Gerut to start the night— which was 54 degrees at game time. It took three pitches for Gerut to make history at Citi Field that could never be erased. They can play for the next 100 years at Citi Field and Jody Gerut will still be the answer to this question. On a 1-1 pitch, Pelfrey served one up to Gerut who slammed one deep down the right field line. With that home run, Gerut not only made Mets history, but he made Major League Baseball history, as well, becoming the first player to open a ballpark with a leadoff home run. What goes along with the territory of leading off the game in a new stadium with a home run is that Gerut—whom no one in San Diego remembers, let alone New York—also gets credit for getting the first hit, the first RBI, and the first run scored. Ironically, 45 years earlier, the last time the Mets opened a ballpark, a visiting player also had the first home run, hit, RBI, and run scored. That player, however, was a future Hall of Famer by the name of Willie Stargell, who has never been confused for Jody Gerut, with all due respect to Gerut. "At Shea, the fan who caught Gerut's homer would have thrown it back," Ben Shpigel wrote in the *New York Times*. "Not here. Too good of a souvenir. The fans unleashed a torrent of boos—even more than descended upon Oliver Perez and Luis Castillo in pregame introductions."

Who was the first Met to hit a homer at Citi Field?

Perhaps no player is more beloved in team history than Mookie Wilson, who played for the Mets from 1980 to 1989 and never stopped smiling for a minute during that time. However, if there is a close second to Mookie—or perhaps even for some ahead of the Mookster—it would be David Wright. The former Mets captain not only was one of the most popular players in franchise history, but he was also one of the greatest players. It is so easy to forget about the numbers that Wright put up from 2005 through 2008. In those four seasons, Wright averaged 29 home runs, 112 RBIs, 41 doubles, and batted well over .300. It was the following season, however, in 2009 when Citi Field opened its doors. Perhaps no player other than the man they would call "Captain America" was more destined to hit the first home run in stadium history for the Mets—in the very first home game played there. That homer came against Walter Silva in the bottom of the fifth inning with two on and two outs. Wright blasted the homer over what would be the short-lived "Great Wall of Flushing." The vast dimensions of Citi Field in its opening year severely hampered Wright's home-run totals but could not stop him from collecting another first in Mets history.

When was the first time the Mets drew more than four million fans in a single season?

One thing is clear: The answer to this question must be a year prior to the time that the Mets moved into Citi Field, which does not have the capacity to allow the Mets to draw four million fans. In fact, the most successful season in terms of attendance in Citi Field history was its very first season, 2009. That year, 3,168,571 Mets fans swarmed to the stadium to see the Mets' new home. The Mets have not approached the three-million mark since. The first time the Mets drew more than three million fans was in 1987 when they drew 3,034,129 to watch the defending world champs. However, only one time did Big Shea have more than four million pass through its turnstiles and that was its very last season. In fact, 4,042,045 fans came to Shea in 2008 to bid farewell to the stadium the Mets had called home since 1964. In that final season, the Mets averaged 49,092 fans per game. The two biggest crowds that season bookended the 2008 campaign. On the final Opening Day at Shea, 56,350 fans packed into the old building for one more opener. On the final day of the season, a disappointing loss to the Florida Marlins, 56,059 showed up to pay their final respects to the building the Mets had called home since 1964. By this point, Citi Field was a hulking presence beyond Shea's left field wall, but it still did not seem real that Shea

Stadium would be gone—to be reincarnated as a parking lot. Yet, the giant horseshoe-shaped stadium had served its time, and more than four million fans got to pay their final respects throughout the year.

What was the first color of the outfield wall at Citi Field?

There were many issues with Citi Field when it first opened in 2009. First, the stadium played way too large and it was almost impossible to hit home runs. This seriously affected the statistics of Mets players, including David Wright, who averaged nearly 30 home runs per season from 2005 to 2008, only to hit 10 in 2009. Most of Wright's power was to right-center field, and at Citi Field, that meant having to hit the ball more than 415 feet. During the 2010 offseason, the Mets began to make major changes in the dimensions of the ballpark, including the height of the outfield walls—which were painted black. Fans were upset that the stadium did not pay homage to its current tenant as much as it did the Brooklyn Dodgers and New York Giants. The black walls with orange trim were reminiscent of the Polo Grounds. However, when the Mets installed new walls—in front of the original walls—they were now Mets Blue. It should be noted that the Mets never removed the original walls, only placed the new walls in front of the old walls. So, if you go to a Mets game today, you can still see the 16-foot-high black wall that became known as the "Great Wall of Flushing" in left field.

Who sang the national anthem at the first-ever game at Citi Field?

The cast of the revival of the groundbreaking Leonard Bernstein-Stephen Sondheim-Arthur Laurents musical *West Side Story*, which had opened on Broadway just days earlier, had the honor of singing the national anthem in front of 41,007 excited New York fans. The cast was headed by Matt Cavenaugh as Tony, Karen Olivo as Anita, Cody Green as Riff, and George Akram as Bernardo. Twenty-one-year-old Argentinian actress Josefina Scaglione costarred as Maria. I'm not saying they were philistines, but there is no chance any player or coach in either dugout knew who any of these singers were. On this night, there would be no rumble—only a disappointing Mets loss.

Who was the manager of the Mets when they opened Citi Field?

Despite opening a shiny, new ballpark, 2009 was not particularly a year to remember for the Mets. After winning the division in 2006 and being in the hunt in 2007 and 2008 under—for the most part—manager Willie Randolph, things did not go as well in 2009. Randolph had been fired for treading water for the first 70 games in 2008 and was replaced by his bench coach, Jerry Manuel. Manuel guided the Mets to a 55-38, second-place finish. In 2009, in that shiny, new ballpark, things were so-so, but Manuel and the Mets struggled terribly on the road, going 29-52 away from Flushing. The team went 70-92 overall and finished 23 games behind the division-winning Phillies. Manuel would only manage the team for one more season, before being replaced by Terry Collins.

Who was the first Mets player to hit a home run into the third deck of Citi Field?

There are quite a few really legitimate guesses that can be made here. The first on your mind might be the Polar Bear himself, Pete Alonso. Alonso has hit a home run into the third deck at Citi Field, but he was not the first to do so. Perhaps you might remember that a visiting player, Aaron Judge of the Yankees, once unloaded on a Robert Gsellman pitch, sending it well into the left field third deck. "Céspedes doesn't even move," SNY announcer Gary Cohen said about the Mets left fielder. That is because—in addition to it being a majestic blast, Céspedes knew what that sort of thing looked like. On June 30, 2016, Yoenis Céspedes became the first player ever to crush a home run into the third deck of Citi Field with a 466-foot blast off the Cubs' John Lackey.

Who was the first pitcher in MLB history to pitch at Citi Field as a member of three different teams within a five-week period? Hint: one of the teams was the Mets.

The 2023 season was anything but a successful one for the Mets and certainly one of the most forgettable ones. Aside from having the opportunity to see some young players come up and show their mettle—pun intended—there were few highlights. Yes, Pete Alonso hit 40+ home runs and drove in 100+ runs for the third time in his five-year career, which

Yoenis Céspedes was the first player to crush a home run into the third deck of Citi Field with a 466-foot blast off John Lackey of the Chicago Cubs in 2016.
IAN D'ANDREA FROM PHILADELPHIA, PA, CC BY-SA 2.0 <HTTPS://CREATIVECOMMONS.ORG/ LICENSES/BY-SA/2.0>, VIA WIKIMEDIA COMMONS

was what the Mets had hoped for going into the season. There were, however, some oddities as well. One of them is the answer to this question—Dominic Leone. When the Mets signed the veteran free agent pitcher—who had pitched for six different teams in his nine-year major league career, the Mets were hoping he would not be the big-league club for too many games. That would signal problems with the Mets' bullpen. Leone pitched in 31 games for the Mets and compiled a 4.40 ERA and a 1-3 record. On August 1, the Mets sent Leone to the Los Angeles Angels in exchange for minor-leaguer Jeremiah Jackson. On August 26, the Angels paid a visit to Citi Field and Leone pitched the bottom of the sixth inning, surrendering a home run to Daniel Vogelbach. However, Leone achieved the hat trick of Citi Field appearances within a five-week period when he arrived in Queens as a member of the Seattle Mariners on September 4. Leone had been waived by the Angels at the end of August and claimed by Seattle. He pitched a scoreless bottom of the fourth inning against his former teammates, twice removed. "I could have just kept my apartment in New York and stayed there," Leone joked with reporters after his final act at Citi Field for 2023.

1967–2023 FIRSTS

THERE IS NO QUESTION THAT 1967 TO 2023 IS A REALLY LONG STRETCH to swatch together in terms of questions. However, if it was broken up into the 1970s, 1980s, 1990s, and so forth, the answers would be much easier to get. This way, you must consider Tom Seaver, Jerry Koosman, Doc Gooden, and Jacob deGrom as possible answers to a pitching question. Same goes for the offensive categories. So, this chapter is going to be difficult, but it is going to truly be for Mets fans of all ages. It levels the playing field, so to speak. By the time you are done reading this chapter, you will be fully caught up on all of the Mets' firsts—not including the postseason, as that is still to come.

The Mets have had their moments—the late 1960s, early 1970s, mid-1980s, late 1990s, early to mid-2000s, mid-2010s, early 2020s. Throughout all of those decades, the Mets continued to pile up firsts. Even 2022, the 60th-anniversary season of the franchise, had some significant firsts—as you will soon read. Just be sure to expand your thought process a bit during this chapter. It is not in order of when things happened, as that too would be making it too easy. Consider all the players that have stood out for the past six decades, as well as those who made a cameo for a first. You need to know your stuff to master this next set of questions. Just how well do you know the Orange and Blue? Good luck!

Who was the first Mets pitcher to earn a save in an All-Star Game?

While it is extremely obvious who the Mets' earliest pitching All-Star was, he is never really thought of as someone who came out of the bullpen, let alone earned any saves. During his 20-year Hall of Fame career, Tom Seaver earned just one regular-season save, and he appeared in a game he didn't start only nine times. However, as a member of the 1967 National League All-Star team midway through his first season in the majors, Seaver earned that save. The game had gone long—real long—and Tom did not appear on the mound at Anaheim Stadium until the bottom of the 15th inning. In the top half of the frame, the National League broke the endless 1–1 tie when Cincinnati star Tony Pérez homered off of Jim "Catfish" Hunter of the Oakland Athletics. It was Hunter's fifth inning of relief work. Seaver jogged in from the bullpen to take the ball for manager Walter Alston and pitched a scoreless 15th inning, striking out one and walking one. The save marked the first of Seaver's 12 All-Star appearances—and was the only time he recorded any kind of decision. "You won the game, you take the ball," the great Don Drysdale told Seaver after the game. Seaver, however, who was mistaken for a bat boy by the clubhouse attendant earlier in the day, handed it back to Drysdale. "No, you take it," Seaver said. "I've got the memories."

Who was the first Met to win a Gold Glove?

The Mets have always been known as a pitching-rich organization, from the late 1960s and early 1970s, to the mid- to late 1980s, to today. Defense, however, has been an on-and-off thing. They have had some unbelievably slick fielders, guys like Keith Hernandez, who might be the greatest fielding first baseman of all time. They had Gold Glove winners that you may have completely forgotten about, like second base winner Doug Flynn in 1980 or center fielder Juan Lagares in 2014. However, the first Gold Glove winner in Mets history is not a surprise, as he is known for making some of the greatest highlight reel catches in Mets World Series history. However, it was the year following the 1969 world title that center fielder Tommie Agee earned the first Gold Glove in franchise history. Two years before arriving in New York, Agee won a Gold Glove as an outfielder for the Chicago White Sox. By winning his second Gold Glove in 1970 for the Mets, he became the first African-American ballplayer to win a Gold Glove in both the American and National Leagues. By the way, Agee also had a magnificent year offensively for the Mets, batting .286, setting then–Mets season records with 182 hits, 107 runs, and 31 stolen bases.

Who was the first manager to have a winning record with the Mets?

Over their first six seasons, the Mets never approached anything resembling a winning record. In fact, the most victories they had achieved over those first years was 66, under second Mets manager Wes Westrum. The Mets grandfather and first manager, Casey Stengel, never had one of his teams win more than 53 games in a season. However, when Gil Hodges arrived to manage the team in 1968, things started to change. While the Mets only managed a 73-89 record in Hodges's first season at the helm, great things were on the horizon. In fact, not only did Hodges become the first Mets manager to have a winning record in 1969, the team won 100 games. It was the first of five straight winning seasons under managers Gil Hodges and Yogi Berra. Of course, those 1969 Mets achieved a whole lot more than a winning record in 1969, but you already knew that.

Everyone remembers the first three Mets broadcasters—Ralph Kiner, Bob Murphy, and Lindsey Nelson, who were in the booth for the team from 1962 to 1978. Who was the first person to replace one of those three legends?

The answer to this question is not Bob Wolff, although the legendary sportscaster did slip into the booth with the Mets' trio to help out on a handful of games in 1978. However, the question clearly asks who was the announcer to replace one of three legends—which happened in 1979, when Lindsey Nelson left the booth at Shea Stadium for good. Replacing him was the youngest member of the Albert broadcasting family, as Steve Albert—brother to Marv and Al Albert—replaced Nelson. By all accounts, including Albert's, it did not go well. He reportedly did not get along well with Ralph Kiner and overall was never accepted by Mets fans. "To be completely honest, I wasn't ready for it," Albert admitted years later. "If I had to do it all over again I might have made a different choice, but you don't know that at the time. I was too young and didn't have the proper experience or the stories that people like Vin Scully and Ralph Kiner had. I just didn't have them yet. It was nobody's fault, I just needed more years in the business before taking on a challenge like that. But it was an opportunity I just couldn't pass up."

Gil Hodges was the first Mets manager to accomplish firsts such as first to win 100 games in a season, first to win a postseason game, and first to win a World Series.

When did the first straight-up trade take place between the Mets and Yankees, where the two teams swapped players?

This one gets a little complicated because there had been transactions between the two teams before they actually traded a player for another player. In June 1966, the Mets purchased the contract of Bob Friend from the Yankees. It was not a trade. In June 1967, the Mets purchased the contract of Hal Reniff. Also, not a trade. In July 1972, the Mets and Yankees were part of a three-team trade along with the Montreal Expos. In that deal, the Yankees sent a player to Montreal and Montreal sent a player to the Mets. Again, doesn't meet the criteria. It was not until December 1977 when the Mets sent Roy Staiger to the Bronx in exchange for Sergio Ferrer. It was less than a blockbuster. Ferrer had seven hits, including a triple, in 40 at-bats following his trade to the Mets. Staiger, a third baseman who was drafted in the first round by the Mets in 1970, hit .226, with four homers and 37 RBIs in parts of three seasons with the club.

The historically pitching-rich Mets have had several pitchers win 20 or more games in a season. The man they called "The Franchise"— Tom Seaver—did it four times between 1969 and 1975. Who was the first Mets pitcher not named Seaver to win 20 games in a season for the Mets?

One year before Tom Seaver won 25 games for the Mets in 1969, his partner-in-crime, Jerry Koosman, won 19 games. Koosman then had to settle for being the 1-A to Seaver. In 1969, Koosman won 17 games— eight less than Seaver—but missed the entire month of June with a hurt arm. He never won more than 15 in a season again—until 1976. One year after Seaver won his 20th game for the fourth time, it was finally Koosman's turn. He won his 20th on September 16 against the St. Louis Cardinals in front of just 5,472 fans at Shea Stadium. Koosman was brilliant, pitching a complete game, giving up just one run on four hits, and striking out 13 Cardinals. "That game stands out as one I will always remember," Koosman said. "I had a great curveball that game. My fast-ball was good, but I had an excellent curveball." Koosman acknowledged that finally getting his 20th win was quite a relief for him personally.

"Absolutely! You know I came close in 1968—I won 19 and had a bunch of games that I pitched at least nine innings and didn't get a run. But certain things happen, and so it goes."

Who was the first player to play for the Mets, Yankees, Giants, and Dodgers?

There are actually three players who share this distinction. None of the three players, however, played for all four teams when they were in New York—that player does not exist. No player ever played for the Mets, Yankees, New York Giants, and Brooklyn Dodgers. The first to ever play for the four franchises, however, was the great Darryl Strawberry. Beginning his career with the Mets, Strawberry won the 1983 Rookie of the Year and was one of the key members of the Mets championship team in 1986. His free agency following the 1990 season was on the front of all of the newspapers in New York City, and, in the end, Tommy Lasorda and childhood friend Eric Davis lured Strawberry out to Los Angeles to play for the Dodgers. That blew up in their faces very quickly, however. In May 1994, Strawberry was released by the Dodgers and picked up by the San Francisco Giants. He played with the Giants sparingly, as his production had gone way down in recent years. Strawberry found new life after returning from a drug suspension in 1995 and joined the Yankees for the final month of the season. He would go on to play for four more seasons in the Bronx, winning the World Series in 1996 and 1999 (Straw missed the 1998 Series while recovering from cancer surgery).

What Mets player ranked first throughout the decade of the 1980s in games, plate appearances, at-bats, hits, doubles, runs, triples, and stolen bases?

You might have thought you had the answer—until you saw that last category the player led. So many candidates for this answer—Keith Hernandez is someone that you can see dominating many of these categories, but triples and stolen bases? No. Darryl Strawberry makes a lot more sense! Alas, the answer to this question is not Strawberry. Then who? Well, one disadvantage for both Hernandez and Strawberry is that they both began their tenure with the Mets in 1983. Mookie Wilson, meanwhile, had a three-year head start on his future teammates and was the top of the pops in all of the listed categories. Mookie, who started with the Mets in the darkest of days, only to be there for the highest of highs, is the only member of the Mets who—during the 1980s—had more than 1,000 games played (the only time a Mets player played in that many games in any decade), more than 4,300 plate appearances (the only time a Mets player had that many plate appearances in any decade), more than 4,000 at-bats (the only time a Mets player had that many at-bats in any decade), and more than 1,000 base hits (the only time a Mets player had that many base hits in any decade). Sounds like more than just a simple compiler, huh? The only category that Wilson led in the 1980s that was close at all was doubles, finishing with one more double than Strawberry.

Who was the first Mets player to win a Silver Slugger Award?

First, it might be necessary to define what the Silver Slugger represents. It is pretty simple: In each league, the best hitter at each position is named as a Silver Slugger. The award was not created until 1980, a season during which there was no chance anyone on the Mets would earn the trophy. In fact, it did not happen until 1984, when Keith Hernandez played his first full season with the Mets. Ironically, it was Hernandez who won the very first National League Silver Slugger Award by a first baseman in 1980 as a member of the St. Louis Cardinals. Now fully ensconced as a member of the Mets, Hernandez hit .311 in 1984, the highest he would hit in his tenure with the Mets. And just one year after Hernandez thought he had been sent to baseball Siberia. "Last year was unique and very unsettling," Hernandez told reporters at the time. "Pressure is not the right word, but when you get traded, you want to do well. Now I've gotten to know the guys, I'm completely adjusted, and happy. It feels like I've been a Met for five years." Of course, 38 years later, Hernandez had his #17 retired by the Mets, making him a Met for life.

Who was the first player for the Mets who stood 6-foot-10 (yes, there was more than one!)?

Let's put things into the proper perspective here—Pete Alonso seems pretty tall, but he is only 6-foot-3. Aaron Judge is a big dude, and probably the first player that comes to mind these days when you think of "tall." Yet, Judge stands just 6-foot-7, three full inches less than the player in question. Back in the day, 6-foot-10 Randy Johnson was extremely intimidating standing on the 10-inch mound. However, the Big Unit never played for the Mets. Eric Hillman, however, did. Hillman, a 6-foot-10 left-handed pitcher, was drafted by the Mets in 1987 and made it to the majors in 1992. Hillman's three-year career with the Mets was less than memorable, as he went 4-14 over the three seasons. He also pitched during a very dark point in Mets history, and actually pitched on the day that his teammate Vince Coleman tossed lit firecrackers into the crowd. "That team was an absolute disaster," Hillman told a reporter years later. "I was 26 and I came up to the big leagues, which had been my dream since I was a little kid. And all I saw were players who were more concerned about their jewelry, their cars and their real estate than the outcome of games." Chris Young—another 6-foot-10 pitcher—hurled for the Mets in 2011 and 2012. However, Hillman was the first.

Who was the Mets' first captain?

Throughout the first 24 years of Mets history, they never had a team captain. Not Tom Seaver, not Jerry Grote, not Bud Harrelson, not Ed Kranepool. In May 1987, while the defending world champions were in a major funk, manager Davey Johnson held a team meeting letting his team know exactly how he felt about the effort that they had been making. To try to spark his ballclub, he named Keith Hernandez, the Mets' fiery leader since mid-1983, as the team's first captain. Hernandez proudly had the letter "C" stitched into the front of his jersey, like a captain in the National Hockey League. Unfortunately, this announcement did not sit extremely well with the Mets' other veteran star, Gary Carter, who was named as co-captain the following season. The pair remained co-captains until they both left the Mets following the 1989 season.

Who was the first major-league slugger to hit his 500th home run as a member of the Mets?

Interestingly, three members of the 28-member 500 Home Run Club at one time or another played for the Mets. However, only one of those three players actually hit the milestone homer as a Met—and he did it against the franchise he started his career with. In addition, this slugger was closely related—literally—to Mets royalty. On April 5, 2009, Gary Sheffield—who is Dwight Gooden's nephew—was acquired by the Mets as a free agent. He had been released by the Detroit Tigers less than a week earlier, sitting on 499 home runs. Twelve days later, he came up as a pinch-hitter for the Mets against Milwaukee Brewers reliever Mitch Stetter. Nine pitches into what would be known as a historic at-bat, Sheffield became the first pinch-hitter to have his first home run with a new team become his 500th career homer. By the way, the other two members of the 500 Home Run Club who at one point played for the Mets were Eddie Murray and Willie Mays.

What was the first uniform number that Dwight Gooden wore for the Mets?

This is a very difficult question since Gooden never actually pitched in a game for the Mets as a rookie in any number other than his famous #16. In fact, he has never been listed as wearing any number except #16 that first year, or in any year with the Mets. However, thanks to a 1985 Topps baseball card set featuring a bunch of rookie prospects, we have photographic evidence that Gooden's originally requested and assigned number with the Mets was #64, paying homage to the year he was born.

When was the first time the Mets made a major change to their original uniforms?

The Mets could not have been much worse in 1978, slogging through the second of what would be four-straight 90-plus loss seasons. So at least they could add a little color to their game—literally. In 1978, the Mets made what would become the first major change to their uniforms. Adding names on the back of their jerseys was still a year away, but that did not stop the Mets from adding some blue and orange bands to the cuffs of their sleeves—and losing the button-up style altogether. In 1978, the home and road jerseys changed from the conventional and historic button-down jerseys to pullover jerseys. These new jerseys had two buttons just below the collar. The blue piping was removed from the road jerseys and blue and orange stripes were added to the cuffs and collar of the shirts. None of these changes, of course, made the Mets play any better, and whether they looked any better was arguable. The Mets would not return to button-down jerseys until the mid-1990s.

Who was the first Mets catcher to receive a no-hitter?

This is a question that many Mets fans once thought would never be asked. How on Earth could a Mets catcher catch a no-hitter? Wouldn't that mean a Mets pitcher would have to pitch one? Of course, all of that changed in 2012 when Johan Santana pitched what has gone down in the record books as the first no-hitter in New York Mets history. Despite the naysayers, Santana's no-hitter is as legit as they come. The controversial fair/foul call down the third base line on a ball hit by Carlos Beltrán would not be reviewable even with the current instant replay rules. To take anything away from what Santana accomplished that night is nonsense and for the most part can be chalked up to non-Mets fans trying to poke the Mets fan. Still, while everyone knows Santana was the pitcher, and that a nondescript outfielder named Mike Baxter saved the day with a brilliant catch in left field, some might forget that Josh Thole was the catcher that night. Ten years later, Thole remembered that a no-hitter was the last thing on his mind heading into that fateful game. "From my vantage point of warming him up and taking him into the game, it wasn't incredibly sharp. We knew we had some work cut out for us," Thole told MLB.com. "When he walked out of the bullpen, I felt like, OK, we're working with the slider right now. It was to that extreme." Santana got his stuff together that night and pitched the Mets' elusive no-hitter. For his part, Thole vividly remembered the end, sort of. "I couldn't wait to turn around and show Gary Cederstrom the ball and be like, 'Just make sure this is strike three,'" Thole told MLB.com in 2022. "When he signaled out, I took off for the mound, and I kind of blacked out after that."

Who was the first player on the Mets to wear uniform #0?

Throughout their 60-plus-year history, the Mets have had five players select to wear #0 on their uniforms. However, to clarify, the four most recent members of that club were really not wearing #0 at all. There was Rey Ordóñez, Omar Quintanilla, Marcus Stroman ('Stro), and Adam Ottavino. You don't have to think too hard to connect the dots on three of those four and Stroman either was playing off 'Stro, or just felt like wearing it, as he kept it when moving on to the Chicago Cubs in 2022. However, none of those players was the first to wear #0, and the chances are, you might not even know the answer after you hear it. Terry McDaniel played 23 games in the major leagues, all with the Mets in 1991, and all wearing #0. McDaniel was drafted by the Mets in 1986, but after five minor-league seasons and 23 games, McDaniel faded into obscurity. One side note: Tony Clark wore uniform #00 for the Mets in 2003, the only player ever to do so.

Who was the first Mets player to homer twice in his very first home game?

Don't think too far back on this one. The first hint for this question is that the home stadium that player hit more than one homer in was Citi Field. The second hint is that it took place in August of the 2022 season. As the Mets were battling for the National League East with the Atlanta Braves, the two teams squared off for a five-game series in early August. Less than a week after acquiring veteran Tyler Naquin from the Cincinnati Reds to bolster their offense down the stretch, Naquin paid immediate dividends. In the opening game against the Braves, Naquin—who had homered only seven times for the Reds in 204 plate appearances—blasted two homers off of Braves starter Kyle Wright, leading the Mets to a 6–4 victory. "It's awesome," Naquin told reporters after his first home game as a Met. "I mean, heck, even if I had been playing here for four years, that's a good night. Very enjoyable. The fans, even from warming up on the line, made me feel right at home."

Who was the most recent Mets first overall number one draft pick?

Throughout their history, the Mets have had the fortune of selecting first overall in the major-league draft. Of course, some might call this misfortune given how bad you need to be in order to get the first overall selection in the draft. In addition, some might call it misfortune after realizing whom the Mets selected with those picks. In 1966, the second year of the MLB Draft, the Mets selected Steve Chilcott first overall. However, plagued by injuries, Chilcott is one of only three players to be drafted first overall and never appear in the majors. The next three top picks for the Mets succeeded to various points. In 1968, they selected Tim Foli, in 1980 they selected Darryl Strawberry, and in 1984 they selected Shawn Abner. However, due to their woeful play in 1993, losing 103 games, they earned the top pick yet again. That 1994 pick is the answer to this question, and that player would be pitcher Paul Wilson. Unfortunately, like most of the Mets' other top picks, Wilson would never attain greatness. Dubbed as a part of "Generation K" by the sportswriters in New York City, Wilson made 26 starts for the Mets in 1996, going 5-12. He would never pitch for the Mets in the majors again. Wilson was decimated by injuries in 1997, 1998, and missed the entire 1999 campaign. During the summer of their championship 2000 season, the Mets sent Wilson to the Tampa Bay (then) Devil Rays for Bubba Trammell and pitcher Rick White. Just as an aside, in his season and a half with the Mets, the journeyman White won more games with the franchise than Wilson did. Wilson, meanwhile, pitched for a few years in Tampa Bay and a few more for the Cincinnati Reds, but never became the pitcher the Mets had thought he would become.

The Mets, as a franchise, have won 11 straight games five times in five different seasons. When did they do it first?

It stands to reason that if a team wins 11 straight games, they are a pretty good team. Rarely do bad teams win that many games in a row. True to that logic, of the five times the Mets have accomplished this feat, three of them were years that they reached the World Series. Two times they actually won the World Series, giving you the answer right there because the Mets have only won the World Series twice—in 1969 and in 1986. In 1969, the Mets not only enjoyed their first winning season and their first 100-win season, but they won 11 straight games stretching from late May into early June. The streak got started following a five-game losing streak, when the Mets defeated the San Diego Padres in walkoff style, 1–0 in 11 innings. The Mets swept the San Francisco Giants and Los Angeles Dodgers three games each to reach seven straight victories, then traveled across the country and swept the Padres in three straight contests in San Diego, before winning the opener in San Francisco for their 11th consecutive win. During the streak, the two Mets aces Tom Seaver and Jerry Koosman were exactly that, as Seaver was 3-0 with a 2.74 ERA and Koosman was 2-0 with a 0.64 ERA. The rest of the pitching staff did their jobs, as well, as the Mets allowed only 64 total hits in 107 innings over the 11 games. It's safe to say that the Mets were streaky in 1969 in the best of ways. In early September, the Mets won 10 straight games and then won nine straight at the end of the season, finishing strong by winning nine of the last 10 games of the season. For the record, the Mets also won 11 straight games in 1972, 1986, 1990, and 2015.

Who was the first Mets player to be inducted into the Hall of Fame?

This is a relatively easy question, especially considering that there are only two players in the Hall of Fame in Cooperstown, New York, donning Mets caps. Mike Piazza, perhaps the greatest power hitter to ever put on the Orange and Blue, with all due respect to Darryl Strawberry and Gary Carter, was inducted into the Hall in 2016—his fourth year of eligibility. However, he was not the first. That honor could only go to one man. He was known as The Franchise, after all. In 1992, Tom Seaver received what was—at the time—the highest percentage of votes to gain entry into the Hall of Fame, appearing on 425 of the 430 ballots (98.8 percent) by the Baseball Writers Association of America. So who were the five who left Seaver off their ballots? Three writers were protesting because Pete Rose was not on the ballot and submitted blank ballots, one was an error of omission, as the sportswriter admittedly overlooked Seaver following a medical procedure, and one writer decided to invent his own rule that he never voted for players appearing on the ballot for the first time. Still,

Seaver received a higher percentage than Babe Ruth, Walter Johnson, and Hank Aaron. It was not until pitcher Mariano Rivera was inducted on all 425 out of 425 ballots that a player surpassed Seaver.

Who was the first Mets batter to hit 50 home runs (or more) in a single season?

The Mets have certainly had their share of power hitters over the years: Darryl Strawberry, Gary Carter, Mike Piazza, Yoenis Céspedes, even King Kong himself, Dave Kingman. However, none of those home-run hitters ever reached the half century mark. That did not happen until 2019 when a hulking rookie named Pete Alonso burst onto the scene at Citi Field. No one had any idea, however, that when Alonso blasted the first home run of the season and his career off of Miami's Drew Steckenrider in the ninth inning that it would be the first of a record-setting season. The rookie record for home runs in a single season had been set just two years earlier by crosstown sensation Aaron Judge. In 2017, Judge blasted 52 home runs to grab the record from Mark McGwire, who hit 49 in 1987. No rookie had ever hit 50-plus homers until Judge and Alonso came along, and no Mets player had ever hit more than 41 home runs—a record that was first accomplished by Todd Hundley in 1996 and matched 10 years later by Carlos Beltrán. On September 20, Alonso smacked his 50th home run of the season off Sal Romano of the Cincinnati Reds. "[Fifty homers] was within the realm of possibility, but I wasn't really shooting for it," Alonso told reporters after the game. "It's tough to wrap my mind around it. I'm just focused between the lines every single day. I don't think this is truly going to settle in until I can sit back after the season." He was the first to accomplish the feat of 50 long balls as a Met; however, he still trailed Judge by two homers for the rookie record with the season winding down. No sweat for the guy they affectionately referred to as the Polar Bear—Alonso hit his 51st homer on September 25 against the Miami Marlins and tied Judge's rookie record with a shot off of Atlanta Braves starter Dallas Keuchel two days later. Wasting no time, Alonso hit the record-breaking 53rd homer of his rookie season off Atlanta's Mike Foltynewicz the very next day. First to 50 as a Met, first to 53 as a rookie. Not too bad for the

24-year-old from Tampa. "I was just overcome with emotion," Alonso told reporters after the game. "I can't describe it. I've never felt anything like that. It was just euphoria and magic. To be a part of Major League Baseball history, to be No. 1 out of every single guy who played the game, it's humbling and it's such a ridiculously awesome feeling . . . that moment was just pure magic."

Who was the first Mets batter to have a 30-30 season (30 homers and 30 stolen bases)?

Major League Baseball's 30-30 Club is one of the most exclusive in the sport. To accomplish such a season, a player must possess power and speed to the extreme. Up until the 1980s, only five men had accomplished this rarest of feats. Bobby Bonds was the king of 30-30, accomplishing the task a remarkable five times—in 1969, 1973, 1975, 1977, and 1978. No member of the New York Mets had knocked on the door of this exclusive club—until 1987, that is. In 1987, not one, but *two* Mets

Pete Alonso became the first Mets slugger to ever hit 50-plus home runs in a season in 2019.
D. BENJAMIN MILLER, PUBLIC DOMAIN, VIA WIKIMEDIA COMMONS

offensive stars made their case for 30-30, and they both actually reached the finish line! Third baseman Howard Johnson and right fielder Darryl Strawberry would both hit 30 or more homers and steal 30 or more bases in 1987. However, Johnson did it just a little faster and became the eighth member of the club. He was also the first National League infielder to ever hit 30 or more homers and steal 30 or more bases. Later in the season, Strawberry became the second Met and 10th overall player to join the exclusive club. HoJo ended his season with 36 homers and 32 stolen bases, and Straw finished with 39 homers and 36 steals.

Who was the first player for the Mets to wear five different uniform numbers in his tenure with the Mets?

Historically, uniform numbers can always conjure up interesting stories for a franchise. For instance, five players wore #41 for the Mets before Tom Seaver came to town in 1967. Of course, no one ever wore it after Seaver, and in 1987 it became the first number retired to honor a Mets player. The second most common uniform number in team history is inexplicably #29, as 42 players have donned that numeral for the Mets (see chapter 4 for the question about the most common number). However, only one Mets player has ever worn five different numbers throughout his tenure with the Orange and Blue. That player is Jeff McKnight, who played for the Mets for a total of just 173 games over a span of parts of four seasons. Still, McKnight managed to wear five different uniform numbers in his time with the Mets. When he joined the team in 1989, McKnight wore #15. Released after that first season, McKnight signed with the Baltimore Orioles and wore two different numbers during two seasons. Not part of the answer, but somewhat interesting. When the Mets re-signed McKnight in 1992, he wore #5. In 1993, he wore the now-retired #17, but switched to #7 during the season. Finally, in his final season with the Mets in 1994, he wore #18. For those keeping score at home, pitcher Ed Lynch wore four different uniform numbers for the Mets during his time with the team in the 1980s, as did pitcher Pedro Feliciano and Kevin Collins, who wore his four numbers for the Mets in a total of just 83 games.

Who was the first Mets player to start at second base for the National League All-Star team since Ron Hunt accomplished the feat back in 1964?

After starting at second base for the National League at Shea Stadium in the Midsummer Classic, Hunt again was named to the All-Star team in 1966. However, he did not start in that game, so this is not in fact a trick question. It would actually take 58 seasons for the Mets to rate another starting All-Star second baseman, and that was Jeff McNeil in 2022. After being an All-Star once before in 2019, McNeil ended up starting the game in 2022 due to an injury to Miami's Jazz Chisholm Jr. "It was pretty incredible, the best baseball players in the world are here and just to be a part of that and start the game was pretty fantastic," he told SNY after the game. "I definitely enjoyed every moment out there." What made it even more special for McNeil was that he was able to start the game at Dodger Stadium, near his hometown of Santa Barbara. "This was the stadium I came to growing up," McNeil told SNY. "I had a blast."

Who was the first player to hit a home run for the Mets and the Yankees in the same season?

The list of players to play for both the Mets and Yankees has gotten quite long over the years. However, there are very few players who have played for both teams in the same season. There are even fewer who have hit home runs for both teams in the same season. In fact, there are exactly two who have done so. The most recent was in 2014, when Chris Young started the season with the Mets, but struggled in his 88 games with the team. He was released by the Mets on August 15. Twelve days later, he signed a minor-league contract with the Yankees. Young spent his first few days as a Yankee in the minors, before being brought up with the September callups. His homer on September 10 put him in the rarest of company. Perhaps no Mets player was as iconic for his home-run blasts in the 1970s as the player known as Kong, Dave Kingman. In 1977, Kingman started the season with the Mets and hit nine homers in 58 games. He was then traded to the San Diego Padres for Bobby Valentine and another player. While in San Diego, the slugger hit 11 homers in 56 games. After being placed on waivers by the Padres

Jeff McNeil, who won a batting title in 2022, was the first Mets second baseman to start an All-Star Game since Ron Hunt did it in 1964.

in September, Kingman was picked up by the California Angels and a little more than a week later was traded to the Yankees. Kingman finally made it to the Bronx on September 17 after playing in only 10 games for the Angels—although he did hit two home runs. In all, Kingman hit 26 homers in 1977 for four different teams—nine as a Met, 11 with the Padres, two in Anaheim, and four more with the Yankees. His first of four homers for the Yankees made him the first player in history to do so for both New York teams in the same season. Kingman would return to the Mets in the early 1980s and hit 72 home runs in three seasons during his second stop in Flushing. In all, throughout his 16-year, 442-home-run career, Kingman homered as a member of seven different major-league franchises.

Who was the first Mets player to have 100 RBIs in a single season?

Despite having some very formidable hitters in the late 1960s and early 1970s, it was not until 1975 that the Mets had a player drive in 100 runs. The final tally that year was actually 105 RBIs, and it was accomplished by one of the most popular players in franchise history—Rusty Staub. In fact, no Met would drive in 100 runs again for another 10 seasons. In 1975, Staub blasted 19 homers for the Mets, 30 doubles, and batted .282. It was the first time Staub drove in 100 runs, something he would only do three times throughout his 23-year career.

Who was the first batter Tom Seaver faced in his return to the Mets in 1983?

The best pitcher to ever don the Orange and Blue, Tom Seaver returned to the Mets following a 5-12 record with the Cincinnati Reds in 1982. When Seaver and the Mets faced one of the best teams in the National League East—the Philadelphia Phillies—to start the 1983 season, it set up a matchup of two all-time greats. Seaver's emotional comeback to Shea started officially when 16-time All-Star Pete Rose stepped into the left-handed batter's box to face the man who years earlier had been dubbed "The Franchise." Seaver calmly climbed to the top of the Shea mound wearing a Mets uniform for the first time in six seasons and struck out Rose swinging. The 55,000-plus fans at Shea roared

One of slugger Dave Kingman's claims to fame is that he was the first player to hit a home run for the Mets and the Yankees in the same season.

with excitement, as Rose glanced out at Seaver while returning to the Philadelphia bench, almost to say, "You still got it."

The first nine people inducted into the Mets Hall of Fame did not enter as players. Who were the first two players inducted into the Mets Hall of Fame?

The Mets Hall of Fame was established in 1981, and after nine members of the Mets front office, broadcast booth, and coaching staff had been inducted, it was finally time in 1986 to add some players. That season, two longtime, popular Mets were enshrined into the Hall—Rusty Staub and Bud Harrelson. Staub had retired from the Mets just one year earlier in 1985, while Harrelson was serving in 1986 as the Mets third base coach. In all, through the 2023 season, 33 men and one woman have been inducted into the prestigious Hall, which first was housed in the Diamond Club at Shea Stadium. When the Mets moved to Citi Field, a large Hall of Fame was opened on the first level of the stadium, within the rotunda. Nine of the 34 members of the Mets Hall of Fame have also been recognized by the National Baseball Hall of Fame in Cooperstown.

What was the first year that the Mets added the players' last names to their uniforms?

Numbers have been on the back of baseball uniforms as far back as 1916, when the Cleveland Indians were inspired by the local football and hockey players wearing uniform numbers. However, it was not until 1960 when the Chicago White Sox became the first team to put players' names on the back of their jerseys. Nineteen years later, in 1979, the Mets had what could best be described as a really bad team. Not in the same way of the early 1960s Mets, but in a much darker, uglier way. The 1979 Mets were just really bad—and often unknown. While the few popular players—like John Stearns, Lee Mazzilli, Doug Flynn, Joel Youngblood, and Steve Henderson—were recognizable, many of the others—such as Dan Norman, Bruce Boisclair, Kevin Kobel, and Sergio Ferrer—were not. So, in 1979, player names were added to the back of the jerseys, "radially arched above the number in blue block letters outlined in orange," according to *Baseball Uniforms of the 20th Century*, written by Marc Okkonen. The names could not help the Mets from losing 99 games that season, however. It was just easier to identify the culprits.

Who was the first Mets pitcher to win 20 games in a single season?

Pretty easy question considering this pitcher was the first, second, and third Mets hurler to win 20 games in a season. However, it was during that magical season of 1969 that Tom Seaver won 25 games, becoming the first pitcher in Mets history to accomplish the feat. Seaver also would win 20 games in 1972 and 1975. Those 25 wins in 1969 also mark the most wins ever by a Mets pitcher during a season. Dwight Gooden came close to the mark in 1985 when he won 24 games. However, it has always been about—and will always be about—Tom Seaver when it comes to Mets pitching leaders. Seaver's 25 wins in 1969 was tops in the majors, en route to his first of three Cy Young Awards.

What was the first Mets team to have six pitchers earn double-digit victories in the same season? Who were the pitchers? BONUS: How many did they each win?

Of all of the firsts, knowing all three of these is quietly one of the rarest and most impressive. Perhaps, just perhaps, the likes of Howie Rose and Greg Prince might give this one a good run. Otherwise, this is PhD-level—not necessarily to guess the year, that's the easy part. However, to guess the pitchers is a lot more difficult and to guess how many each pitcher won is nearly impossible—nearly. First of all, you have to have a team that wins a heck of a lot of games during the season—like 108, for example. OK, that part of the question, the easy part, is that it was accomplished in 1986. Now, for those responsible. It's really no surprise that the Mets top four starters each won 10 or more games. Bob Ojeda actually led the team with 18 wins, Dwight Gooden earned 17 wins, Sid Fernandez won 16 games, and Ron Darling had 15 wins. No surprise with any of those statistical accomplishments. What is unique is that swingman starter and reliever Rick Aguilera won 10 games of his own. Then, the most surprising of them all. Very rarely, if ever, does the man who leads your team with 22 saves also win 14 decisions; however that is exactly what Roger McDowell did in 1986. Long before McDowell became known as the "Second Spitter," he turned in a 1986 for the ages. For good measure, Jesse Orosco—who saved 21 games for the Mets in 1986—won eight games of his own. "When attempting to build a starting rotation, a front office needs to think of employing five men who complement each other," Mets blogger Tim Boyle wrote in 2018. "A variety of skills, handedness, and other factors should be taken into account. In 1986, the Mets had about as ideal of a rotation as you will find in baseball."

Who was the first Mets player to win a batting title?

While the Mets had always had some really great hitters, none of them had been able to finish the season in the top spot when it came to batting average. Part of that was a result not of Mets not having high batting averages, but a testament to other hitters in the National League. In 1969, for instance, Cleon Jones hit an incredibly impressive .340 for the season. However, that was good for only third in the National League, behind Pete Rose's .348 average and Roberto Clemente's .345. The one that is really hard to believe was the 1998 season, when John Olerud set a New York Mets franchise record with a .354 batting average. However, that was the same year that Colorado's Larry Walker batted an incredible .363 for the season. Sure, Walker was playing in Coors Field, but the record does not make a provision for that. Olerud finished second in the batting title race. It was not until 2011 when José Reyes, the slick-fielding shortstop, had the offensive season of his career, batting .336—third best in franchise history. Reyes finished just ahead of Milwaukee's Ryan Braun, who finished the year at .332. It was a bittersweet time for Mets fans, however, as Reyes—the highly popular player—was never offered a contract with the Mets following the season. Instead, the batting champ signed a six-year, $111 million deal with the Miami Marlins. Years later, Reyes admitted he never wanted to leave the Mets, but without a contract offer he had little choice but to sign with Miami. Reyes eventually would return to the Mets for the 2016–18 seasons and would once again become a fan favorite. Since retiring, he has been seen many times taking in Mets games at Citi Field. He also participated in the Mets reboot of Old-Timers' Day in August 2022.

Who was in the first class inducted into the Mets Hall of Fame?

There was really no hard decision in 1981 when the Mets opened their Hall of Fame, which sat within the Diamond Club at Shea Stadium, as to who the first two inductees should be. No two people were more influential in the early days of the franchise than owner Joan Whitney Payson and legendary manager Casey Stengel. "A lifelong baseball fan, Joan Whitney Payson became the first woman to purchase a major sports team when she bought a majority stake in the expansion franchise that became the Mets in 1962," it reads on the Mets Virtual Vault webpage. "Payson was no absentee owner: she took an active role

José Reyes was the first Mets player ever to win a batting title when he did so in 2011. He was also the first Met to bat at Citi Field.
JEFFREY HAYES, CC BY 2.0 <HTTPS://CREATIVECOMMONS.ORG/LICENSES/BY/2.0>, VIA WIKIMEDIA COMMONS

in the running of the team and became a familiar and beloved presence to players and fans alike." The second person inducted into the Mets Hall was Stengel. "When the Mets first took the field in 1962, they were led by the inimitable former New York Yankees skipper Casey Stengel. An icon in the Big Apple, Stengel warmed the hearts of Mets fans with his 'Stengelisms' while trying to coax wins from his overmatched expansion team," it reads on the Mets Virtual Vault site. Of course, hiring Stengel was a stroke of brilliance by Payson, as the larger-than-life character was able to deflect all of the pressure—and what otherwise might have been negative attention—from the players. He was a grandfatherly figure, who was as equally beloved as the team itself.

Who was the first Cy Young Award winner for the Mets?

A question about Mets pitching firsts? The answer is almost always Tom Seaver. However, in this case the answer is—well, Tom Seaver. In 1969, there was little competition for the man they called "The Franchise" as his 25-7 record, his 2.21 ERA, and his 208 strikeouts made him a runaway winner for the National League Cy Young. He received all but one of the votes, with one voter opting for Phil Niekro. What is almost more impressive is that Seaver was almost named as the National League's Most Valuable Player. Seaver received 72 percent of the vote, just behind the winner Willie McCovey, who garnered 79 percent. Despite winning three Cy Young Awards throughout his career, 1969 was the closest he ever got to winning both of the major awards in the National League. Apropos of pretty much nothing, it is worth noting that Seaver earned $37,500 for the 1969 season. If you do the fancy math, that is equivalent to about $315,000 in 2023 money. To say the least, a club-friendly contract.

Who was the Mets' first player-manager?

This is another case of first and only, and you can add extremely short-lived. Former St. Louis star Joe Torre had joined the Mets in 1975 and batted over .300 in 1976, but was off to a slow start in the 1977 season. In fact, the entire team was off to a slow start that season, prompting the Mets to fire their manager, Joe Frazier, in May. The team

Tom Seaver accomplished more firsts than any other member of the Mets. There is a reason that he is known as "The Franchise."

named Torre, who had played in the big leagues for 18 years and had a well-respected baseball mind, as its player-manager. That lasted just 18 days, however, before Torre decided to retire fully as a player so that he could focus on the managing job. His final at-bat came on June 17, 1977, when he put himself in as a pinch-hitter. As a full-time manager, however, the early reviews were early raves for Torre. "The way the Mets have played the past week, it is apparent that Joe Torre is some kind of drug," sportswriter Murray Chass wrote in the *New York Times*. "The instant Torre became the new manager a week ago, the Mets inhaled him, they smoked him, they shot up with him—whatever it took to get Torre and his enthusiasm and his intelligence into their veins." After winning six out of seven in early June, even Mets general manager Joe McDonald was singing the praises of Torre. "In the history of baseball," he told reporters, "you have to wonder if a manager was able to turn on as many guys as Joe Torre did six or seven days ago." Of course, the good vibes wore off pretty quickly, as the 1977 Mets went on to finish with a record of 49-68 record under Torre, and 64-98 overall. The following seasons did not yield much better results for Torre, whose Mets went 66-96 in 1978, 63-99 in 1979, and 67-95 in 1980. Of course, Torre would go on to win a total of 286 games as the manager of the Braves, Cardinals, Yankees, and Dodgers, and earn a plaque in Cooperstown for his managerial career. His time as skipper of the Mets is not mentioned in the narrative of his Hall of Fame plaque. Still, he got his first managing gig with the Mets and was their first player-manager.

Who pitched the first no-hitter for the Mets?

For the purpose of this answer, know this—Carlos Beltrán's ball was called foul by the third base umpire. There was no instant replay in 2012. Had there been, Beltrán's ball would not have been reviewable. A ball that is called fair or foul by a base umpire before it reaches the base is not a reviewable call. So to say that the Mets' first no-hitter is not legitimate, is actually, not legitimate. For more than 100 years umpires have made safe-out calls, fair-foul calls, ball-strike calls, and they stand as called. In the top of the sixth inning on that night, Beltrán fouled a ball off before grounding out to third base. OK, back to that night in June 2012: Mets broadcaster Howie Rose—who knows more about the New York Mets than any other person who has ever lived—said early on in the broadcast, "And if you think tonight's going to be the night, forget it." Santana was returning from shoulder surgery and manager Terry Collins was very clear that he would not allow Santana to go too far in the game. "There were a lot of questions about his pitch count, and all of the questions to Terry before the game was how long he was going to let Johan go.

He told us 110 to 115 tops and we took that as gospel." It wasn't. Every no-hitter seems to have a defensive play that defines it, and in this game that came in the top of the sixth inning when left fielder Mike Baxter robbed Yadier Molina of a hit, crashing into the wall and separating his collarbone. "A ball that off the bat, your instinct is it's catchable. And it was. No-hitter or no no-hitter, you're out there trying to make plays," Baxter told reporters. Santana did the rest and finished it off by striking out David Freese, on his 134th pitch of the 8,020th Mets game. "The whole atmosphere in the ballpark—how it goes from just another game, regular game early, to a playoff atmosphere? At that point, to celebrate this game like you won the whole thing, it was really nice," Santana said. "It was one of the best memories I ever had as a baseball player."

Johan Santana famously—and somewhat controversially—pitched the first no-hitter in Mets history in 2012.
USER TEDKERWIN ON FLICKR (ORIGINAL VERSION) USER UCINTERNATIONAL (CROP), CC BY 2.0
<HTTPS://CREATIVECOMMONS.ORG/LICENSES/BY/2.0>, VIA WIKIMEDIA COMMONS

Who was the first 79-year-old pitcher to take the mound for the Mets in front of nearly 40,000 fans at Citi Field?

Well, admittedly, this is sort of a trick question since the game against the Amazins' and the Miracles was not technically an official game. However, when Steve Dillon took the mound for the fourth time as a member of the Mets, it was very memorable. Originally drafted by the New York Yankees out of Cardinal Hayes High School in the Bronx, Dillon pitched in just three major-league games during his brief tenure with the Mets in 1963 and 1964. Very rarely does a player have a 58-year hiatus from the game before making a "comeback." Yet there he was, the Long Island southpaw making his way to the mound at Citi Field during the Mets Old-Timers' Day Game in August 2022. Following his time with the Mets, Dillon went on to serve with the NYPD for 20 years. However, he had one more mound to climb. The Mets had not had an Old-Timers' Day since 1994—30 years after Dillon threw his final pitch as a big leaguer. Yet, when he slipped into his uniform and approached the mound to face Mookie Wilson, he was ready. "I prepared myself for this," Dillon said after the game. "The last thing I wanted to do was embarrass the Mets, and embarrass myself, and embarrass my family. Meeting the new players and having them embrace me was an experience that I'll never forget."

Who was the first member of the Mets to lead the league in stolen bases?

The Mets had a short list of base stealers throughout their history. The speedy Mookie Wilson was probably best known through the 1980s, and guys like Howard Johnson and Vince Coleman and even Lance Johnson and Roger Cedeno had memorable stolen base years for the Mets. However, none of them ever led the National League. That honor would not come until 2005, José Reyes's first full season in baseball. He stole 60 bases that year, but would improve on that total in the next two seasons. In 2006, Reyes led the majors with 64 stolen bases and in 2007 once again was the best in all of baseball with 78 steals. When he became the first Mets player to lead the National League in steals, he

Carlos Beltrán, one of the Mets' best all-time players, was famously on the other side of a Mets first—Johan Santana's no-hitter.
KEITH ALLISON ON FLICKR (ORIGINAL VERSION) UCINTERNATIONAL (CROP), CC BY-SA 2.0 <HTTPS:// CREATIVECOMMONS.ORG/LICENSES/BY-SA/2.0>, VIA WIKIMEDIA COMMONS

beat out Florida Marlins speedster Juan Pierre by just three swipes. By 2007, he had 14 more steals than Pierre.

Who was the winning pitcher in the first-ever regular-season inter-league game between the Mets and Yankees?

In 1997, the Mets were not sporting one of the best rotations in team history. Hard-working starters with limited talent and potential seemed to litter the roster, guys like Rick Reed, Bobby Jones, and Mark Clark. Then, there was a 29-year-old right-hander named Dave Mlicki, who was acquired from the Cleveland Indians following the 1994 season to try to strengthen the Mets rotation. It was Mlicki who got the call in the first-ever "Subway Series" regular-season game against the Yankees on June 16 at Yankee Stadium. The Yankees were the defending World Series champions. The Mets were not. Still, on any given day—and this one happened to be in front of 56,188 screaming fans in the Bronx. "I took a walk out to Monument Park before the game, just to try and get a sense of the stadium and I got goosebumps. When the schedule came out before the season started, that was a date I circled that I wanted to pitch," he said years later. Mlicki got his wish, and made the most of it, pitching a complete-game shutout against the Yankees, striking out eight batters en route to victory. "We were absolutely the underdog and really weren't supposed to do anything," Mlicki said. "They were the defending champs. At the time, I knew that it was big, but I didn't know how big. In fact, it didn't really hit me until days later, and it was such a cool feeling. It was awesome."

Who was the first member of the Mets who hailed from Alaska?

Anchorage, Alaska, is 4,373 miles from Flushing, Queens. However, that is not the exact route that pitcher David Williams took to the Mets. In addition to being the first player from Alaska to play for the Mets, he was also the first player to come out of Delaware Technical and Community College in Dover, Delaware. Now, how DTCC knew to scout a pitcher from Anchorage is one thing; having him ascend to the majors just a few years later is another entirely. I am sure the DTCC scouts and coaching staff very much enjoyed their reindeer hot dogs on their visit to the great state of Alaska, but they really didn't have much time to get to know Williams. By the age of 19, he was drafted and playing for Erie of the New York–Penn League. He worked his way to the majors by 2001 with the Pittsburgh Pirates, was traded to the Cincinnati Reds for Sean Casey in 2005, and to the Mets in 2006. The Mets used Williams sparingly during their National League Eastern Division championship year. Williams appeared in six games for the Mets that regular season, going 3-1. He was not on the Mets' postseason roster in 2006 but returned in 2007 to pitch in two games for the Mets, battling various injuries. He was released following the season, going on to pitch for a few seasons in Japan and in the Washington Nationals organization. Williams is not only the first player from Alaska to play for the Mets, but—by default—is the greatest Mets player ever who was born in Alaska. No other Alaskan natives have ever played for the Mets.

When was the first time the Mets pitched a combined no-hitter?

The 2022 Mets accomplished more than a few goals and objectives. One of the most impressive early in the season was when five, count 'em, *five* Mets pitchers combined to no-hit the division-rival Philadelphia Phillies, who went on to win the National League pennant. On April 29, Tylor Megill got the start for the Mets and pitched for five innings, throwing 88 pitches, striking out five, and walking three batters. Drew Smith, Joely Rodríguez, and Seth Lugo then came on in relief to do their jobs—pitching one inning apiece. Then, the ball was handed to closer Edwin Díaz for the ninth inning, who struck out the teeth of the Phillies' order in Bryce Harper, Nick Castellanos, and J. T. Realmuto in the ninth. Catcher James McCann relied on calling mostly sliders from Díaz, who was not at all surprised. "In the bullpen, it was nasty. I knew he would call the slider a lot because I'm facing the heart of the order," Díaz told reporters after the game. In all, Mets pitchers threw 159 total pitches, struck out 13 batters, and walked six.

When was the first time the Mets scored 12 runs in an inning?

In 2016, the defending National League champions had their moments where it looked like they wouldn't be able to score 12 runs in a week. However, there were also flashes of the incredible en route to the playoffs for the second-straight year. The biggest of those flashes took place on Friday, April 29, against the San Francisco Giants. Little did everyone know what was about to occur when they moved to the bottom of the third inning against Giants starter Jake Peavy in a scoreless game. In that third inning, the Mets would pound out seven hits, including a grand slam and six RBIs from Yoenis Céspedes. "This is a different team, for sure," Mets manager Terry Collins told reporters following the game. "You just go through those streaks sometimes where it doesn't matter what you do, you can't score. Tonight, we swung the bat and it seemed like everything we hit, it went into a gap somewhere." Mets pitcher Steven Matz said thank you very much and held the Giants down for the 13–1 victory. Unfortunately for the Mets, the Giants would have the last laugh, defeating the Mets in the winner-take-all Wild Card Game at the end of the 2016 season.

Who was the first member of the Mets who was born and raised in Flushing, Queens?

Well, the answer to this question actually holds more significance than simply being the answer to this question. Hang on, that will make sense in a minute—I think. On October 11, 1947, Charlie Williams was born in Flushing—15 years before the Mets were a franchise. Then, on June 7, 1968, he was selected by the Mets in the seventh round of the free agent draft. He went on to pitch just one season for the Mets, posting a 5-6 record in 1971. So here is where things get a little more interesting with the Charlie Williams story. Early in the 1972 season, Williams was traded to the San Francisco Giants—straight-up—for Willie Mays. Williams went on to pitch for seven seasons with the Giants as a serviceable reliever. So not only is he the first player to play for the Mets from Flushing, Queens, but he is also the only player ever to be traded for the great Willie Mays, whose number was retired forever in Flushing in 2022.

Who was the first infielder to win a Gold Glove for the Mets?

There are some really good options for this question on its face, as the Mets have had a lot of Gold Glove winners, particularly among their infielders. Keith Hernandez won six straight Gold Gloves for the Mets at first base and shortstop Rey Ordóñez won three straight during his time with the Mets. Even second baseman Doug Flynn, who arrived in New York as part of the dreaded Tom Seaver trade, won one. However, the first-ever Gold Glove for a Mets infielder went to one of the most popular Mets of all time—Bud Harrelson, who won the National League

Gold Glove at shortstop in 1971. It was the second overall Gold Glove for the Mets, one year after center fielder Tommie Agee won his award. Harrelson was epic in 1971, committing just 16 errors on 714 chances in 140 games—a fielding percentage of .978. That season, not unlike his entire career, the sure-handed Harrelson turned difficult and extremely hard-hit grounders into what appeared to be easy outs. However, injuries plagued Harrelson for much of his career, and the two-time All-Star rarely played a full season for the Mets after 1971.

Who was the first Japanese-born ballplayer to play for the Mets?

Many would answer this question quickly and confidently say that the answer is Hideo Nomo—and they would be wrong. The great Hideo Nomo pitched for the Mets starting in 1998, and was early-on certainly the best-known Japanese-born player to play for the Mets, but there was actually one player who predated Nomo. In May 1997, left-handed relief pitcher Takashi Kashiwada made his debut for the Mets. Prior to coming to the Mets—and the United States—Kashiwada pitched for the Yomiuri Giants. Before coming to the Mets, Kashiwada had won only one game with Yomiuri, but actually went 3-1 with the Mets. However, his stay in the majors was a short one. Following the 1997 season, he returned to the Yomiuri Giants and became a lefty specialist out of the bullpen. In 1998, the Mets added two new Japanese pitchers to their staff—the aforementioned Nomo, as well as Masato Yoshii. However, there can only be one first and that will forever be Takashi Kashiwada. PS: Kashiwada also is the first Japanese-born ballplayer to ever bat for the Mets, striking out in his only plate appearance for the team.

In 2022, which Met hit a home run on his very first major-league swing?

"I'm here for a reason," the Mets rookie said prior to his first-ever major-league start. "I'll let it show." He did indeed. After taking ball one in his first at-bat against the Atlanta Braves, Brett Baty launched a curveball from Jake Odorizzi over the right field wall to become the first Mets player in 17 years to homer in their first at-bat. Not only his first at-bat, but his very first swing, the day after the 12th overall pick in the

2019 Draft and the Mets' second-ranked prospect was promoted to the bigs. In front of his parents, family, friends, and thousands of Mets fans who made the trip south, Baty made it a most-memorable night. "I was just looking for a pitch to drive," Baty said through a big smile to reporters following the game. "He left one over the plate, so I was just looking to get it up in the air and I did. It was awesome."

When was the first time a Mets team finished a season with a winning record?

On September 9, 1969, the Mets and Cubs squared off against one another with a pitching matchup for the ages. Perhaps in 1969 no one realized just how significant this night game at Shea Stadium would be in the annals of the Mets. Perhaps they did. One thing the more than 51,000 fans knew as they packed into Shea Stadium was they were going to be watching two of the greatest in the game at the moment. It would take years to realize they were two of the greatest to ever live. Tom Seaver entered the game for the Mets with a record of 20-7. Ferguson Jenkins entered the game with a record of 19-12 for the Cubs. Yet, it was the Mets bats that stole the show, scoring seven times against Jenkins and the Cubs, as the Mets went on for the 7–1 victory. This was far from the end of the 1969 National League East pennant race, which still had a few weeks of amazing-ness to go. However, this victory was the Mets' 82nd of the season, clinching the first winning season in franchise history. There would be 18 more regular-season victories, of course, along with seven more in the postseason. However, at this moment, on this night, the Mets—for the first time ever—were no longer going to finish a season with a losing record.

Who was the first Mets player to be named MVP of the All-Star Game?

Even though this former Rookie of the Year and Mets Hall of Famer is one of the greatest players in the history of the franchise, he is often overlooked. However, pitcher Jon Matlack made sure to make the most out of his selection to the 1975 All-Star Game. The Mets southpaw pitched two scoreless innings for the National League and ended up being the game's winning pitcher. He ended up sharing the award with a guy who had just about the closest thing to the same name as Matlack, without having the same name. Bill Madlock helped lift the National League to victory with his two-run double against Goose Gossage in the ninth inning. Just in time for Matlack to get the win—and share the MVP honors.

Who was the first player to ever start for the Mets on Opening Day and then never play another major-league game?

Opening Day at Shea Stadium in 1983 was one of the most memorable in history because that was the game that saw the return of Tom Seaver to Flushing. However, it ended up to be just as memorable for a young outfielder by the name of Mike Howard, who started in right field for Seaver's comeback game. Having played a handful of games during the 1981 and 1982 seasons for the Mets, Howard had a batting average of just .125 in his career. However, in the bottom of the seventh inning against future Hall of Famer Steve Carlton, it was Howard's base hit that gave the Mets a 1–0 lead against the Philadelphia Phillies. He had no putouts or assists in right field that day for the Mets, or any other day for that matter. The Mets would soon call up Darryl Strawberry to be their right fielder, and Howard had no place to play. There was talk of converting him to catcher, but that never happened. Instead, he became one of only three players in the history of Major League Baseball since World War II, according to the Elias Sports Bureau, to have his team's season opener be his last-ever major-league game. Howard spent the rest of the 1983 season in the Mets' minor leagues and the 1984 season in the Pacific Coast League, as a member of the Pirates' Triple-A squad. They even tried him as a pitcher, to no avail. "Howard went into a funk after being demoted, hitting below .200 at Triple-A. He was sent to rookie ball with the intent of adding catcher to the list of positions he could play. (Howard played every one, including pitcher, at some point in his pro career.) But the Mets didn't recall him," sportswriter Mark Simon wrote for ESPN.com in 2011.

The Mets made several trades at the start of the 1980s that were integral to their success later in the decade. Which one of these came first?

1. Lee Mazzilli sent to the Texas Rangers for Ron Darling and Walt Terrell

2. Gary Carter acquired from the Montreal Expos for Hubie Brooks, Mike Fitzgerald, Floyd Youmans, and Herm Winningham

3. Keith Hernandez acquired from the St. Louis Cardinals for Neil Allen and Rick Ownbey

4. Sid Fernandez acquired from the Los Angeles Dodgers for Bob Bailor and Carlos Diaz

It is hard to state just how important all four of these trades were for the Mets, as they looked to move from cellar dwellers to eventual world champions. Each of these trades provided the Mets with key pieces of what would become the 1986 Mets. Which trade started the ball rolling, however? Well, the answer is definitely not Gary Carter, who arrived as the "final piece of the puzzle" during the 1984 offseason from Montreal. Just months earlier that summer, Carter had the opportunity to catch Mets rookie phenom Dwight Gooden at the MLB All-Star Game. The two joked about how great it would be to get to work together every day. Beginning in 1985, that joke was no joke—it was an incredible reality. Thanks to Carter's veteran leadership behind the plate, Gooden—who won the Cy Young Award—had one of the greatest seasons a pitcher has ever had, going 24-4, with an earned run average of 1.53. Both Hernandez and Fernandez arrived in Queens in 1983. The St. Louis Cardinals, for an assortment of reasons, were looking to move the former batting champion and co–National League MVP and were more than happy to take relievers Neil Allen and Rick Ownbey. Off-the-field transgressions were later revealed as part of the backstory, but the Mets would not have changed a thing. Hernandez went on to become one of the greatest and most beloved members of the Mets—and deservedly had his #17 retired during the summer of 2022. Six months later, in December 1983, the Mets made a trade with the Los Angeles Dodgers to acquire the large lefty, El Sid Fernandez. They sent Bob Bailor, a veteran infielder, and Carlos Diaz, a young pitcher, back to Los Angeles. Fernandez would go on to be an extremely popular member of the Mets and a key to the championship team in 1986. However, all three of those trades followed the answer to this question, and perhaps one of the greatest trades in team history—although at the time, it was not a very popular one. On April 1, 1982, Brooklyn's own Lee Mazzilli was dealt to the Texas Rangers. The lone star for many years on a starless team, matinee idol looks and all, Mazzilli was shipped off to the Lone Star State for two young pitchers—Ron Darling and Walt Terrell. When Joe Torre was fired as the team's manager, it seemed to be a fait accompli that Mazzilli could be sent packing. First, there were a lot of right fielders on the Mets at the time—none particularly good, but all possibly a little better than Mazzilli. "He is a symbol, he has made a significant contribution to the Mets, but he did not figure to get much playing time with the club in 1982," Mets general manager Frank Cashen told reporters. Mazzilli was disappointed, but not disillusioned. "There's more behind this," he told reporters, "I'm part of the old regime. I have been here the longest. I'm a little too big in New York, too." In the end, the trade meant more for the 1986 Mets than any other could, especially because of the cherry on top—hang on a sec for that. The trade in 1982 for Darling and Terrell, would—in reality—become a trade for Darling and infielder Howard Johnson, whom the Mets acquired for Terrell in the winter of 1984. Both Darling and HoJo would become extremely valuable members of the 1986 championship team, as well as for years to follow. But that wasn't the cherry on top—in August 1986, as the Mets were enjoying their magical season—they reacquired a veteran outfielder who had spent the past few years with the Texas Rangers, New York Yankees, and Pittsburgh Pirates. That player's name was Lee Mazzilli. So, in the end the Mets traded Mazzilli for Darling, HoJo, and Mazzilli? Not exactly, but close enough.

What Mets player hit a game-winning, walkoff home run in his very first game as a member of the Mets?

There is a lot more to this walkoff homer than meets the eye—mostly because of the pitcher who gave up the home run. The pitcher was former Mets reliever Neil Allen, who was traded by the Mets to the St. Louis Cardinals two seasons earlier for a first baseman by the name of Keith Hernandez. Allen had been a good relief pitcher for the Mets from 1980 to 1982, saving 59 games for a team that did not win many games, However, he was the key piece, along with fellow reliever Rick Ownbey, to be sent to St. Louis for Hernandez. That is what made Gary Carter's at-bat versus Allen in the bottom of the 10th inning during Opening Day of 1985 so ironic. Carter ripped an Allen offspeed pitch into the Cardinals bullpen to give the Mets a walkoff victory. Safe to say that Cardinals manager Whitey Herzog and Hernandez did not celebrate after the game over a Budweiser.

When was the first time the Mets played a regular-season game that was not played in the United States or Canada?

Many people remember the Mets playing a two-game series against the Chicago Cubs in the Tokyo Dome in 2000. However, that was not the first time the Mets traveled internationally to play a regular-season game. On August 16, 1996, the Mets opened a three-game series against the San Diego Padres in Estadio de Béisbol Monterrey in Monterrey, Mexico. It marked the first time that any Major League Baseball team played a regular-season game in Mexico. In front of more than 23,000 fans—the biggest crowd ever in the stadium for any event—the Mets dropped that first game to the Padres, 15–10. Despite scoring 10 times, the Mets hit only one home run in the game, and that was hit by the often-forgotten and almost never-remembered Andy Tomberlin. The Mets would win their first-ever international game the next night against the Padres.

Who was the first Mets pitcher to win a Silver Slugger Award?

It seems to be an oxymoron—the best-hitting pitcher would get something called the Silver Slugger Award? Well, until the 2022 season,

Many felt Hall of Famer Gary Carter was the "final piece" needed for the Mets to win a world championship.
SCOTT CUNNINGHAM, PUBLIC DOMAIN, VIA WIKIMEDIA COMMONS

when the National League permanently added the designated hitter once and for all, each season a National League pitcher would be named as its league's best hitter by position. Since this award began being handed out in 1980, long after the American League adopted the DH, no American League pitcher was ever awarded a Silver Slugger. But we digress. The Mets always had some good-hitting pitchers. Take Walt Terrell, for example, a rookie who arrived with the Mets in 1982 from the Texas Rangers, along with another good-hitting pitcher, Ron Darling, in exchange for Lee Mazzilli. Terrell actually blasted two home runs in one game for the Mets in 1983. What made that unique feat even more impressive was that Terrell hit the homers against future Hall of Famer

Ferguson Jenkins of the Chicago Cubs. Terrell homered for a third time later that season and managed a batting average of .182 and drove in eight runs. He did not, however, win the Silver Slugger that season. A member of the Mets pitching staff would not win a Silver Slugger until nine years later when, in 1992, Dwight Gooden took the honor. In 1992, Doc batted .264, with a home run, a triple, and three doubles. He also had nine RBIs and had a total of 19 hits.

Who was the first Mets batter to collect six hits in a single game?

It took 37 years for a Mets player to accomplish this feat. There had been plenty of five-hit games by New York batters, but it was not until August 30, 1999, that Edgardo Alfonzo went 6-for-6 against the Houston Astros. Along the way, Fonzie hit three homers, drove in five runs, and scored six runs in the Mets 17–1 laugher against the Astros. Alfonso got things going early, hitting a solo homer off of Shane Reynolds in the top of the first inning. In the top of the second, he singled, and blasted a two-run homer in the top of the fourth. In his fourth at-bat in the top of the sixth inning, Alfonzo hit his second home run of the game. However, Fonzie was far from done. In the top of the eighth inning, he singled to lead off the frame and because the Mets scored so many runs, he got a sixth at-bat in the top of the ninth inning—during which he slapped an RBI-double, completing his 6-for-6 night, setting a Mets record with 16 total bases along the way.

Who was the first Mets batter to hit a home run from both sides of the plate in a single game?

There are several impressive feats when it comes to hitting home runs from both sides of the plate in a single game for the Mets. For example, Carlos Beltrán did it five different times while playing for the Mets. José Reyes, in 2003, became the youngest player to ever accomplish the feat at the age of 20 years and 78 days. However, the man who did it first for the Mets was their star from the late 1970s with matinee-idol looks—Lee Mazzilli. Perhaps the most impressive part of Mazzilli's achievement was that he did it in a ballpark that is not exactly home run friendly. On September 3, 1978, the Mets traveled across the country to Dodger

Stadium in Los Angeles. Mazzilli wasted little time getting going on what would be a very big day for him—leading off the top of the first inning from the right side against lefty Tommy John. Mazzilli blasted his 15th homer of the season to deep left to give the Mets a 1–0 lead. Mazzilli faced John during his next two at-bats, singling both times. Then, in the top of the seventh inning against right-handed reliever Charlie Hough, Mazzilli turned around to bat left-handed. It mattered little on this afternoon, as Maz ripped a deep home run to straight-away center field for his second home run of the game. Overall, Mazzilli went 4-for-5 with the two homers and three RBIs.

When did the Mets first set the dubious modern major-league record of having batters hit by a pitch the most times in a season?

It's a painful record to have—and no one really wants it. The Mets, however, as of the 2022 season, own the mark for most hit batsmen in a season. The record-setting 106th hit batter occurred in the ninth inning of the Mets' loss to the Brewers at American Family Field. The victim? Luis Guillorme's left foot. That moved the Mets past the 2021 Reds, who were hit by 105 pitches to set the modern record (since 1900). The 1889 Orioles hold the overall record with 160 hit batsmen. "I don't really know what to think of it," Mets outfielder Brandon Nimmo told reporters after the game. "Teams are having to try and figure out ways to get us out. I guess that's part of the way—they're trying to pitch inside, so you're going to get hit when that happens." For the Mets, 2022 was a season-long hit-by-pitch. The trend of hit batsmen resulted in everything from multiple benches-clearing fracases, to players being hit in the face, to a handful of injuries over the course of the summer, not the least of which was when Starling Marte was hit in the hand, causing him to miss important games down the stretch.

What was the first Mets team to hit eight home runs in a single game—the most in franchise history?

On August 24, 2015—one of the most memorable stretch months in Mets history—the team traveled to Philadelphia for a Monday evening contest. By the end of the game, the Mets had barraged Phillies pitching with 16 runs on 20 hits—eight of which were home runs. This in a game that Jacob deGrom suffered through one of his worst career outings, giving up seven runs on eight hits in just 2⅔ innings. The offense would erase any discussion about the Mets' pitching, however. Things started innocently enough in the top of the second inning, with the Mets already trailing by a score of 3–0. David Wright stepped to the plate for the first time since April 14 against Adam Morgan. Wright had missed nearly the entire season due to injury. It mattered little. Wright absolutely crushed a 1-1 pitch to deep left field for a dramatic home run. "David Wright brings himself back to the lineup with thunder!" Mets television announcer Gary Cohen exclaimed. "Holy smokes, the Captain is back," Mets radio voice Howie Rose shouted. It turned out that the David Wright drama was just the start. In the top of the third inning, trailing 4–1, Juan Lagares homered to left. Then, in the top of the fourth inning, Wilmer Flores and Travis d'Arnaud hit back-to-back homers to bring the Mets to within 7–5. In the top half of the fifth inning, Flores smacked his second home run of the night and two batters later, Michael Cuddyer finally gave the Mets the lead with a blast to deep left-center. The Mets had more to come, however, as Daniel Murphy homered in the top of the sixth inning to put the Mets ahead, 10–7. In the top of the ninth inning, Yoenis Céspedes ripped a two-run homer to left field, giving the Mets eight home runs in a single game for the first time.

In a late-September game in 2022 against the Miami Marlins, the Mets reached a franchise first by pretty much not doing anything at all. What was it?

Jon Heyman, a baseball columnist for the *New York Post* and an insider for MLB Network, tweeted about this incident in about the funniest way I saw. He seemed to grasp the stupidity of the actual baseball aspect and add some laughs along the way. "Note out of the Marlins clubhouse: Richard Bleier is believed to be the first Jewish player to be called for three balks in one inning on Rosh Hashanah." That's right, three balks, three—not just in one inning, but during one at-bat—leading to a run and some really angry Marlins. The Mets—and Pete Alonso—purely by accident and umpire arrogance, became part of history, as this was the first time since pre-1900 in Major League Baseball that a pitcher balked three times during a single at-bat. Bleier, who had pitched for seven years in the majors, making 303 appearances, had never before balked. Never. Yet, first base umpire John Tumpane had issues with the way Bleier was not coming to a complete stop—and let him know about it three times. By the end of the inning, Bleier and Marlins manager Don Mattingly were tossed for arguing what was truly a bizarre circumstance. The final balk brought in a run, although the Mets ended up losing the game and the balks were more spectacle than anything else. "Words cannot describe what happened in that inning on my end," Bleier said after the game.

When was the first time the Mets led off a game with three straight home runs?

The Mets had, in fact, gone back-to-back-to-back several times throughout their history, but it was not until October 4, 2022, that they accomplished that impressive trio-feat to start a game. Facing the Washington Nationals in the second-to-last game of the 2022 season, and in the second game of a doubleheader, Brandon Nimmo led off against Washington's Paolo Espino. It was the second game of a doubleheader, so Nimmo was hardly seeing his first pitch of the day. In game one, he had gone 3-for-5, with a home run and three RBIs, leading the Mets to their 99th victory of the season. Facing Espino, Nimmo launched a deep blast to right-center field on the second pitch he saw for a majestic home run, landing in the Mets' bullpen. The next batter was Francisco Lindor, who swung at a 2-2 pitch from Espino and deposited it in the second deck of the Coca-Cola Corner. The next batter was Jeff McNeil who, not to be outdone, crushed a 2-0 pitch even deeper into the second deck than Lindor for the Mets' third straight homer to start the game. The milestone home-run record, while coming in the Mets' 100th win of the season, proved to be bittersweet, as it was also on this night that the Atlanta Braves won their 101st game of the season to clinch the National League East.

Who was the first player to play for the Mets that was born in the 2000s?

The Mets, throughout their history, have always had some of the highest touted prospects in all of baseball. How those prospects would perform when they arrived in the majors, however, was another story entirely. Early in the Mets' history, it was always interesting to note when a player on the team was born after the team was created. In other words, if a player was born in 1962 or 1963, the Mets' first two seasons, they would have come up to the majors, theoretically, in the early 1980s. However, this question may make some Mets fans feel even older than that. The first Mets player born in the 21st century was actually born on November 19, 2001, and made his major-league debut on September 30, 2022, as a 20-year-old, highly touted prospect. Unfortunately for Francisco Álvarez, that debut game didn't really go as planned. In Atlanta for the most important series of the 2022 regular season, Álvarez was thrust into the DH role and looked, at times, overmatched. Alvarez went 0-for-4 with one strikeout, but nothing could dampen the smile on his face that he had finally arrived in the big leagues. Of course, moving forward, most if not all of the Mets arriving in the majors will have been born in the 2000s. However, it is Álvarez who can claim to be the first. Speaking of firsts, he hit the first home run of his career a few games later at Citi Field, making him the first Met born in the 2000s to hit a home run!

Who was the first Met to hit into four double plays in a single game?

To be fair, this was all Félix Millán's fault. On July 21, 1975, against the Houston Astros, the Mets steady second baseman had a really good day at the plate, going 4-for-4 with four straight singles. However, Millán's strong day of consistent hitting was at fault for causing one of the worst offensive days for the man hitting right behind him—Joe Torre. The die seemed to be cast in the very first inning against pitcher Ken Forsch. Torre stepped up to the plate following Millán's first hit and promptly tapped back to the mound for the 1-4-3 double play. Inning over. In the bottom of the third inning, Del Unser and Millán singled for the Mets with one out. That brought up Torre, who slapped a grounder to Houston shortstop Roger Metzger, who started the 6-4-3 double play. Three innings later, Millán led off for the Mets with a single, followed by Torre grounding to the second baseman, Larry Milbourne, for the 4-6-3 twin-killing. Three at-bats for Torre, three groundball double plays. In the bottom of the eighth, Torre accomplished something that no other major leaguer had done in 100-plus years and something that no one on the Mets had ever done—he grounded into yet another double play. Unser reached on a bunt single, Millán singled—again, and again—Torre grounded into a 6-4-3 double play. "I'd like to thank Félix Millán for making this all possible," Torre told reporters after the game. "He ought to get an assist."

Who was the first Mets player to enter the Hall of Fame in Cooperstown wearing a Mets cap on his plaque?

It is not always the case that the best ever was the first ever—not by a longshot. However, for this question, that is absolutely the case. On August 2, 1992, George Thomas Seaver was inducted into the Hall of Fame, having been elected with a then-record 98.84 percent of votes. There was never any doubt which cap would reside on Seaver's plaque—despite the fact that he pitched a no-hitter during his time with the Cincinnati Reds and won his 300th game as a member of the Chicago White Sox. Seaver was the Mets, and the Mets were Seaver: case closed.

Who was the first pitcher to throw a no-hitter against the Mets and then later in his career pitch for the Mets?

It is not very often that your team can get no-hit, by a future Hall of Famer no less, and have it just be another game. That is how it felt on that October night at Citi Field, as the Mets were on their way to a division title and, ultimately, the National League pennant. Of course, no one knew those things would happen when they faced off against the Washington Nationals and their ace, Max Scherzer. Earlier in the 2015 season, Scherzer had pitched a no-hitter against the Pittsburgh Pirates, the first of his career. However, on this night he was as dominant as any pitcher could be, mixing up his fastball and slider to strike out 17 batters. Oh, and he did not walk anyone. The only baserunner permitted by Scherzer was Mets catcher Kevin Plawecki, who reached on a throwing error. Daniel Murphy later reached base on a fielder's choice in that same inning. "At times, Scherzer looked as if he was simply playing catch with Wilson Ramos. Wherever Ramos put his catcher's mitt, Scherzer seemed to hit it," the Associated Press story about the game read. It was considered one of the most dominant pitching performances in history. The Mets, prior to the 2022 season, were hoping that Scherzer just had some of that dominance still in that right arm, when they signed him to a three-year, $130 million deal. "Max is one of the greatest pitchers of this and any generation," Mets owner Steve Cohen said at the press conference to introduce Scherzer. "He is a Hall of Famer who knows how to win, and that's a great quality to add to the clubhouse, too. Now we get to pair Max with one of the other great generational pitchers, Jacob deGrom. I told you last year I wanted to win, and I talked about sustained winning and winning championships, and I mean it. And I think the Mets today are closer to that than we were then. We are a better team today than we were two weeks ago." There was absolutely no question that the final part of Cohen's statement was true, as Scherzer had a terrific campaign in 2022, propelling the Mets to 101 regular-season victories. However, things did not end well for the ace, who found himself getting booed off the mound at Citi Field after failing in Game 1 of the National League Wild Card Series against the San Diego Padres. Unfortunately for Scherzer and the Mets, he had his worst outing of the season at the worst possible time. Of course, things would get worse between the Mets and Scherzer in 2023, leading to the Mets trading him to the Texas Rangers at the trade deadline.

Who was the first Mets pitcher to lose both games of a doubleheader?

Doug Henry didn't spend very much time with the Mets as a relief pitcher, but was on the team long enough to have a Mets first—even if it is not a good one. After pitching well for the Mets out of the bullpen in 1995, Henry really struggled out of the bullpen during the 1996 campaign. Never was that more evident than on July 23, when bad pitching and bad luck conspired against him. In game one of a doubleheader at Coors Field in Colorado, Henry walked two and gave up two RBI singles to get tagged with the loss. In the nightcap, he allowed a walkoff single to Eric Young Sr., which gave the Rockies an 11–10 victory. Overall, Henry went 2-8 for the Mets in 1996 with nine saves. He was released by the Mets following the season.

The Mets have had two players enter the Baseball Hall of Fame wearing a Mets cap—Tom Seaver and Mike Piazza. However, they have had 13 other Hall of Famers play for them over the course of the players' careers. Who was the first player who played for the Mets to be inducted into Cooperstown?

Among the players who played for the Mets in their early days were some of the greatest players to ever live: Warren Spahn, Duke Snider, and Willie Mays, just to name a few. However, the first player to be inducted into the Hall of Fame that also played for the Mets is actually known much more as a manager for the team. However, after playing 18 seasons for the New York Yankees—and winning 10 world championship rings—Yogi Berra came out of retirement to play four games for the Mets in 1965. He would return to manage the Mets when Gil Hodges died suddenly before the start of the 1972 season. That same summer was when Berra would be enshrined in Cooperstown, along with Sandy Koufax and Early Wynn. The following season, Berra and the Mets won the National League pennant, but after losing to the Oakland Athletics in the 1973 World Series, there were not many bright spots for Berra and the Mets. He was fired midway through the 1975 season.

In July 2023, which Mets player became the first player in franchise history with two triples in the first three innings of a game? As a bonus, in the same game, this player became the first at his position in major-league history to have a five-hit game that included two triples and a home run. Name him.

After having an up-and-down first two seasons in New York, Francisco Lindor—at times—looked like the player the Mets thought they were getting when they traded for the All-Star after the 2020 season. It was in that July game against the Arizona Diamondbacks that Lindor showed what he was truly capable of. He started his big day in the top of the first inning, by ripping a triple to right field in front of a Pete Alonso homer. In the top of the third inning, Lindor took Ryne Nelson's pitch deep to left-center—the ball cleared all of the outfielders and Lindor raced to third for his second triple of the game. In the top of the fourth inning, Lindor went 3-for-3 when he grounded a base hit in the hole between first and second—however he was hardly finished. In the top of the sixth inning, Lindor launched a 400-plus-foot homer to right-center field, giving the Mets a 9–0 lead and Lindor a 4-for-4 night. Lindor would have one more at-bat—and singled to complete the record-setting 5-for-5 day. It was one of the few bright spots for the Mets in a summer of horrors.

WHO DID IT FIRST?

THIS IS A FUN-LITTLE SECTION OF THE BOOK TO BRING TO LIGHT SOME of the great individual achievements by many past Mets, with the onus on you to decide "Who Did It First?" These questions will span the decades and answers may come from any Mets era. In this chapter you actually will be given the answer to every question—you will just have to decipher which of the other choices are incorrect. Sometimes having the answer right in front of you makes the question easier—but sometimes it is absolutely no help at all! Please note that these questions are in no particular order, or logical timeline. Here goes!

Who was the first Mets slugger to smack 40 or more home runs in a single season?

1. Pete Alonso   2. Todd Hundley   3. Carlos Beltrán
4. Mike Piazza

Only four Mets have ever hit 40 or more home runs in a single season, and all four of them are on this list. Pete Alonso is the only person to do it twice and is also the only player to ever hit more than 50 homers in a season for the Mets. That, of course, came during his magical rookie season of 2019, when Alonso blasted a major-league record 53 homers. However, Alonso was far from the first to hit 40 for the Mets. In fact, when Todd Hundley hit his 41 home runs—the most ever by a catcher—Alonso was only two years old. In 1996, Hundley hit his then major-league-record-setting 41st home run of the season, passing Dodgers great Roy Campanella. It was the most home runs ever hit by a Met—a mark that was tied by Carlos Beltrán in 2006. Mike Piazza fell one homer short of the team mark in 1999, when he hit 40. "I feel like 1,000 pounds have been lifted off my shoulders," Hundley told reporters after the game. "I'm relieved more than anything. There was no doubt I was going to get it. It was just, when? This is like Christmas morning when you want to open the gifts and get it over with. Patience is not one of my strong points."

Who was the first Mets pitcher to pitch a complete game?

**1. Tom Seaver   2. Jay Hook   3. Roger Craig
4. Jon Matlack**

The Mets' first complete game, as documented earlier in this tome, came on the very day the Mets earned their first franchise victory. Starting pitcher Jay Hook figured he would kill two birds—or Pirates, in this case—with one stone. He mixed up his three pitches well, and defeated Pittsburgh 9–1 at Forbes Field. He even held future Hall of Famer Roberto Clemente hitless. "The main thing I remember was that if we would have lost one more, it would have been a record opening the season, and if Pittsburgh won one more, they would have had the record for wins," Hook said recently. "I had pitched one game before that, and we had been winning in that one, but they took me out and we ended up losing. This time, I pitched a complete game." The game ball is now in the Hall of Fame in Cooperstown.

Who was the first Mets pitcher to strike out the first eight batters he faced to open a game?

**1. Tom Seaver   2. Jacob deGrom   3. Jerry Koosman
4. Pete Falcone**

This absolutely sounds like something that Tom Seaver could have and should have done at some point during his legendary career. After all, Seaver did strike out 19 in a game once, and he did strike out 10 in a row once. However, he never struck out the first eight batters of a game. Neither did Jerry Koosman nor Pete Falcone. That honor goes to Jacob deGrom, who struck out the first eight Miami Marlins he faced during the latter part of his rookie season in 2014. In what may well have been foreshadowing for his future, he did not get a decision when Jeurys Familia blew the save and the Mets lost the game. Back to deGrom, though. He struck out Christian Yelich, Donovan Solano, and Casey McGehee in the top of the first inning; Marcell Ozuna, Justin Bour, and Adeiny Hechavarría in the top of the second; and caught Jordany Valdespin and Jeff Mathis looking in the top of the third, to tie the major-league record for most strikeouts to start a game. In 1986, Jim Deshaies accomplished the feat for the Houston Astros. Then, perhaps the strangest part of this story took place. Needing one more strikeout to own the record by himself, and facing the opposing pitcher, Jarred Cosart—a journeyman pitcher who had seven hits in five years—deGrom surrendered a ground-ball single to right field. DeGrom ultimately pitched seven innings and struck out what was at the time a career-high 13 batters. For the record, Pete Falcone did strike out more than 100 batters per season in three of his four years with the Mets, so let's show him some respect.

Who was the first Met to leg out 20 or more triples in a single season?

**1. José Reyes   2. Mookie Wilson   3. Lance Johnson
4. Ángel Pagán**

The answer to this question really should be José Reyes, but it's not. Reyes led the team in triples six times and actually led the majors in triples four times. However, one thing Reyes never did was reach the 20-triples mark in a single season. His highest mark was 19 triples in 2008. Mookie Wilson, for all his speed and stolen bases, never had more than 10 triples in a season, and Ángel Pagán topped out with 11 for the Mets, although he did lead the majors with 15 as a member of the Giants in 2012. That leaves Lance Johnson, who only played one full season for the Mets, but certainly made his mark. In 1996, Johnson—who had 117 triples in his 14-year career—legged out 21 triples for the Mets. He became the first Mets hitter to reach 20 triples, and he is their all-time single-season triples leader.

Jacob deGrom was the first Mets pitcher to strike out the first eight batters he faced to open a game.

Who was the first Mets batter to hit .300 or higher in a single season?

1. Joe Christopher   2. Joe Torre   3. Joe McEwing
4. John Olerud

John Olerud certainly set a standard that has been not only unmatched but not approached by any other player in team history. His .354 batting average in 1998 is 14 points higher than Cleon Jones's .340 in 1969. However, Olerud was not the first Mets player to crack .300. That honor goes to a player who has yet to be mentioned in this book so far, and was an original Met, selected fifth in the 1961 expansion draft from the Pittsburgh Pirates. Joe Christopher had never played a full season in the majors, let alone bat close to .300 entering the 1964 season. However, it was in fact Christopher who had a career year in the team's first season at Shea Stadium, slugging 16 homers, driving in 76 runs, while legging out 26 doubles and eight triples. All of these heroics allowed him to go 163-for-543—a batting average of exactly .300184. In this case, however, .300 will suffice. Christopher is often forgotten by fans because he got injured the next season and never again put up the kind of numbers he did in 1964.

Who was the first Mets manager to notch 500 wins with the team?

**1. Gil Hodges   2. Bobby Valentine   3. Terry Collins
4. Davey Johnson**

Other than Gil Hodges, whose career—and life—was cut tragically short in 1972, all of the managers on this list won more than 500 games for the Mets, and all of them managed the team for seven seasons. That, in itself, will give you the answer—given that Johnson managed the team before Valentine, who managed it before Collins. Not only did Davey Johnson reach the 500-win mark first as a Mets manager, but he has more wins than any manager in franchise history with 595. Collins is second with 551 wins, followed by Bobby V., who won 536 games. In addition, Johnson—who managed the Mets from 1984 to 1990—had a winning percentage of .588 during his tenure, winning one championship, one National League pennant, and two division crowns.

Who was the first Mets batter to walk five times in a single game?

**1. Mike Baxter   2. Daniel Murphy   3. David Wright
4. Vince Coleman**

This is an oddity that has only happened twice in the history of the Mets, and the man to do it first was not exactly known for his discerning eye at the plate. In addition, you may decide to put an asterisk next to this answer, although it is the absolute correct answer. In 2012, Mike Baxter was best known for the leaping catch he made in left field to save

Joe Christopher was the first-ever member of the Mets to bat .300 or better. He did so in 1964, when he also hit 16 homers, drove in 76 runs, and ripped 26 doubles.
UNITED PRESS INTERNATIONAL, PUBLIC DOMAIN, VIA WIKIMEDIA COMMONS

Johan Santana's no-hitter—the first in franchise history. Baxter crashed into the left field fence and ended up on the injured list. However, later that season, Baxter returned to draw five walks against the San Diego Padres in five plate appearances, tying a franchise record. The first man to walk five times in a game for the Mets—as improbable as it sounds—was free-swinging Vince Coleman, who did it exactly 20 years earlier in 1992. The only thing is, Baxter accomplished his five walks in a nine-inning game in five plate appearances. Coleman's official record came in a 16-inning loss to the Pittsburgh Pirates. And three of those walks were intentional. Still, Coleman's mark is recognized as tying a then National League record. In fact, walking five times in a single game is rarer than pitching a no-hitter, or hitting three home runs in a single game. For his career, Coleman had a walk rate of less than 8 percent, but on this day in 1992, he was destined for the record books—almost involuntarily.

Who was the first Met to drive in nine runs in a single game?

**1. Carlos Beltrán   2. Carlos Delgado   3. Carlos Baerga
4. Carlos Gómez**

Here is a hint—the answer to this question has the first name of Carlos. Did that give it away? It is possible, in fact, that any of these Carloses drove in nine runs in a single game for the Mets; however, only Carlos Delgado accomplished this lofty feat—which is a franchise record for runs batted in for a game. To make the accomplishment even more satisfying for Mets fans, Delgado had nine RBIs in a single game against the Yankees—at Yankee Stadium, no less. Coming into the game on June 27, 2008, Delgado was scuffling, going just 2-for-22—and had only 35 RBIs for the entire season. However, he was about to bust out. In the top of the fifth inning, facing Yankees rookie starter Dan Giese, Delgado ripped a two-RBI double deep down the right field line. In the next inning, facing Yankees reliever Ross Ohlendorf with the bases loaded, Delgado smashed a grand slam home run deep to right-center field to give him six RBIs on the night. With the Mets leading the Yankees 12–5 in the top of the eighth inning, Delgado came to the plate against LaTroy Hawkins with two runners on and crushed another homer to right field. That gave Delgado nine RBIs for the game. "What can I tell you? I came in here pretty pumped up about this series and had a good game," Delgado told reporters after the game. Yankees manager Joe Girardi, meanwhile, was a little more to the point: "Delgado killed us today," he told reporters.

Who was the first Mets pitcher to pitch for a last-place team and finish first in the National League in earned run average?

**1. Tom Seaver   2. Craig Swan   3. Kevin Kobel
4. Frank Viola**

At first consideration or contemplation, almost every pitching question in this book has a chance to legitimately have Tom Seaver be the answer. In fact, Tom Seaver led the National League in ERA three times during the 1970s, but alas—go figure—none of those teams finished in last place. Most of Craig Swan's teams, however, did actually finish in last place, including the 1978 season, when Swan led the National League with a 2.43 ERA. How bad were the Mets that year? Swan had a record of only nine wins and six losses to go along with that splendid earned run average. As a team, the Mets' ERA was 3.87 that season, with the team going just 66-96. The record should also show that Kevin Kobel, who was a relief pitcher for the Mets in 1978, finished the season with an ERA of 2.91 in his 32 appearances.

Who was the first Mets batter to hit in 30 straight games?

**1. Moisés Alou   2. Hubie Brooks   3. David Wright
4. Mike Piazza**

By 1984, Hubie Brooks was already established as a fan favorite when he hit in 24 straight games. His 33 hits during the streak raised his average from .203 to .306, and he hit two home runs and drove in 10 runs during that stretch. Following that season, Brooks was included in the trade that brought Gary Carter to the Mets from Montreal. Fifteen years later, in 1999, Mike Piazza also hit in 24 straight games, raising his average from .314 to .326, hitting eight homers and driving in 18 runs. It was Moisés Alou, however, during the painful collapse of 2007, that set a team mark by hitting in 30 straight games. During that time, Alou had three three-hit games, four home runs, and 16 RBIs. He raised his batting average from .313 to .344. Not only was this the first—and only time—a Mets batter hit in 30 straight games, it was also the longest hitting streak for a player north of age 40. "I remember being locked in. But the thing that I'm most proud about with that 30-game hitting streak is the period of time when it happened," Alou told blogger Matthew Brownstein of Metsmerized Online in 2020. "We were in the pennant race and to be hot and getting hits every day during that race is something that I'll always be proud of."

Who was the first Mets pitcher to have an ERA under 2.00 for a single season?

**1. Dwight Gooden   2. Jacob deGrom   3. Jerry Koosman
4. Tom Seaver**

You ask, and you ask, and you ask, and—at some point, the answer needs to be Tom Seaver. In this case, it is. In 1971, Tom Seaver had one of the greatest seasons of his career—and it is never, ever talked about. People talk about 1969, when Seaver won 25 games and the Cy Young Award; they always bring up 1973, when Seaver won 19 games, and his second Cy Young Award; even 1975, when the team was terrible, but Seaver was brilliant—winning 22 games and his third Cy Young Award. However, in 1971 Seaver was outstanding, going 20-10 with a microscopic 1.76 earned run average, the best in all of baseball. He also led the National League with a personal-best 289 strikeouts, but finished second in the Cy Young voting to Fergie Jenkins, who won 24 games but had an explosive ERA of 2.77. Well, explosive compared to Seaver that season. Just to round out the question, Gooden had a 1.53 ERA in 1985, deGrom had a 1.70 ERA in 2018, and Koosman had a 2.08 ERA in 1968.

Who was the first player to appear in 12 Opening Days for the Mets?

**1. David Wright   2. Tom Seaver   3. Bud Harrelson
4. Ed Kranepool**

This is a close one, as Bud Harrelson appeared in 11 straight Opening Day games from 1967 to 1977. That became the Mets' all-time record in 1977, as his good friend and teammate, Tom Seaver, did not pitch in his first opener until 1968. Seaver was traded during the 1977 season, leaving Jerry Koosman to start the opener in 1978 and halting Seaver at 10 Opening Days. That all changed, however, in 1983 when Seaver made his return to the Mets and pitched in an extremely memorable Opening Day—his last as a member of the Mets. So Seaver and Harrelson were tied for the most Opening Day appearances in franchise history with 11—until 2016. Back in 2005, David Wright was in his first full season with the Mets. He had played 69 games for the Mets in 2004 and impressed people enough that he would be the Opening Day third baseman in 2005. He would not relinquish that role over the next 12 seasons, becoming the first Mets player ever to appear in 12 openers. Only injuries conspired to end Wright's streak, as the Mets' captain missed the entire 2017 season with an injury and returned for just two symbolic games in 2018. The frustration in 2017 was real and obvious. "After 12 straight starts at third base on Opening Day to begin his major league career, Wright will be reduced to a spectator when the Mets play their opener against the Braves at Citi Field," Mets beat writer Mike Puma wrote in the *New York Post* the day before the game. "He will still be in uniform for pregame introductions and then will watch from the dugout." No other Mets player has ever reached double digits in openers.

Who was the first Mets pitcher to strike out every batter they faced during an All-Star Game?

**1. Dwight Gooden   2. Jacob deGrom   3. Jon Matlack
4. Johan Santana**

This one appears, initially, to be an easy answer. Most Mets fans remember that Dwight Gooden burst onto the scene as a rookie in 1984 and made a splash at the Midsummer Classic at Candlestick Park in San Francisco. Gooden came into the game in the top of the fifth inning and promptly struck out Lance Parrish, Chet Lemon, and Alvin Davis. Following the final strikeout, Montreal catcher Gary Carter pumped his fist toward Gooden as he ran to the dugout, where Gooden received a hero's welcome. However, that is all that most of us remember about Gooden on that night. The truth is, he came back out to pitch in the top of the sixth inning—Lou Whitaker grounded back to the mound, Eddie Murray blooped a double behind shortstop, Cal Ripken Jr. grounded out to third, and Dave Winfield flew out to left field. An amazing performance by the 19-year-old phenom. However, it is not the answer to this question. Despite highlight reels showing just the three up, three down strikeouts from Gooden, there was that top of the sixth. In 2015, a young pitcher by the name of Jacob deGrom took the mound at Great American Ballpark in Cincinnati for his first All-Star appearance. DeGrom had won the Rookie of the Year Award one year earlier in 2014, but was not well known throughout the majors. That all changed in Cincinnati. In the top of the sixth inning, deGrom struck out all three batters he faced on just 10 pitches. The hitters—Stephen Vogt, Jason Kipnis, and José Iglesias—never had a chance against deGrom, who was lauded by FOX Sports play-by-play man Joe Buck after the inning: "Hi, I'm Jacob deGrom," Buck said, as deGrom walked off the mound, "and I have the chance, with my stuff, to just dominate baseball for years to come."

Dwight Gooden held many firsts for the Mets, and had an iconic All-Star Game appearance in 1984 as a rookie.
JEFF MARQUIS, CC BY 2.0 <HTTPS://CREATIVECOMMONS.ORG/LICENSES/BY/2.0>, VIA WIKIMEDIA COMMONS

Who was the first Mets player to play in all 162 games of a season?

**1. John Olerud   2. Rusty Staub   3. Félix Millán
4. Francisco Lindor**

In his very short time with the Mets, John Olerud left his mark in many ways. In his first two seasons with the team, he played in 154 and 160 games. In 1997, after signing with the Mets as a free agent, he batted .294, with 22 home runs, 34 doubles, and 102 runs batted in. The following season, in 160 games he batted a franchise-best .354, with 22 home runs, 36 doubles, and 93 runs batted in. However, in his third—and final—year with the Mets, he was a true iron man, leading the entire major leagues by playing in every single one of the Mets' 162 games. He is one of only two Mets to accomplish this incredible mark of durability, but he was not the first. Twenty-four seasons earlier, in 1975, 31-year-old Félix Millán was about as reliable as players get. Millán led the majors by playing in all 162 of the Mets games—and many of those games were hard to watch, let alone from the second base position. Millán's steadiness was realized at the plate and in the field. The career .279 hitter batted .283, with a then franchise best 37 doubles and a then franchise record 191 hits. He also continued to be the toughest batter to strike out in all of the National League.

Who was the first Mets player to have a 100 percent success rate in stolen bases (with at least 20 attempts)?

**1. José Reyes   2. Kevin McReynolds   3. Carlos Beltrán
4. Mookie Wilson**

This one is going to surprise you, as it is not someone who was known for being a speedster with the Mets. He was, however, one of the most successful base stealers in team history percentage-wise. Yes, José Reyes will most likely always be the Mets' stolen base king. From 2005 through 2008, Reyes stole 60, 64, 78, and 56 bases. He also led the league two of those seasons getting caught stealing. That is not incredibly surprising; if you are going to attempt a steal, at some point you are going to get thrown out. Unless your name is Kevin McReynolds, who combined a lot of power with some sneaky speed and some even sneakier stolen bases. Never known as much of a base stealer while with the San Diego Padres, McReynolds packed his running shoes when he arrived in New York. In 1987, his first year with the Mets, McReynolds blasted 29 home runs, had 32 doubles, drove in 95 runs, and stole 14 bases in 15 attempts. Pretty good, huh? The following year, however, as the Mets were heading to the National League East crown, McReynolds even outpaced himself. The slugger—and speedster—batted .288, with 27 homers, 30 doubles, 99 RBIs, and 21 steals. Here is the thing though: he never got caught stealing—for the entire season. McReynolds was successful 21-out-of-21 times. Those who know math really well can confirm that is a percentage of 100 percent! Actually, people who cannot even spell the word *math* would know that it was 100 percent. His 21 straight steals set a major-league record, which would last until 2009.

Who was the first Mets player to earn more than $1 million in a season?

**1. George Foster   2. Keith Hernandez   3. Tom Seaver
4. Bobby Bonilla**

In 2022, the Mets paid Max Scherzer $43.3 million, Jacob deGrom $35.5 million, and Francisco Lindor $34.1 million. Forty years earlier, in 1982, the Mets total payroll was just over $3.5 million. More than just a little inflation. In fact, using a run-of-the mill inflation calculator on the internet, you will find that the $3.5 million in 1982 is worth around $10.7 million in 2022.

In 1981, Mike Jorgensen was the highest paid player on the Mets roster by making $800,000 for the season. However, in 1982 the Mets were ready to break the bank on a superstar. That superstar was Cincinnati Reds slugger George Foster. The Mets gave Foster the largest contract in their 20-year history—$1.6 million per season for five years, with an option for two additional years. The deal also called for a $1 million signing bonus—not something the Mets had gotten used to giving players. So, after signing that deal, Foster became the first million-dollar man for the Mets. It would take until 1984 when Keith Hernandez made just over $1 million that the Mets had two players who made above the million-dollar mark. For all of the money Foster was able to deposit in his account at Manufacturers Hanover, he never produced on the field for the Mets. In 1982, Foster batted just .247 and hit just 13 homers. Although his power numbers would improve over the next few seasons, they would never approach the success or the statistics that Foster had with the Reds, and he was released midway through the 1986 season.

ADMITTEDLY IMPOSSIBLE QUESTION—I would say possibly 1 percent of Mets fans would know the answer to this question. Do you? We ask it more because the answer is so strange. No uniform number has been worn more than #6, as 44 different Mets have donned the numeral. In 2022, Starling Marte wore #6 after three years of it being worn by Jeff McNeil. Here is the real question—who wore it first?

**1. Lou Klimchock   2. Cliff Cook   3. Jim Marshall
4. Rick Herrscher**

Here is one thing that is for sure, it is not Lou Klimchock, who played for the Mets—and wore #6—in 1966. This question was included in the book not so that it could be answered, although that would be incredible, but because of the absurdity of the answer. Alas, all three other men on the list, Cliff Cook, Jim Marshall, and Rick Herrscher, all played for the Mets in 1962 and all of them wore #6. The correct answer, however, is Jim Marshall, who played with the Mets before being traded on May 7 for a guy by the name of Vinegar Bend Mizell. On that same May 7, the Mets sent Don Zimmer to the Cincinnati Reds for Cliff Cook, who was assigned uniform #6 by the Mets' clubhouse attendant. In his three and a half years with the Reds, Cook had worn four different uniform numbers, but never #6. He was soon sent to the minor leagues. Two weeks later, the Milwaukee Braves sent Rick Herrscher to the Mets. #6 was available, so of course it was assigned to him—the third player in two months to wear the number. Throughout Mets history, #6 has been worn multiple times during a season, multiple times. In 1990, three different Mets—Mike Marshall, Darren Reed, and Alex Treviño—wore the number. In 2004, four different Mets—Ricky Gutiérrez, Jeff Keppinger, Gerald Williams, and Tim Wilson—wore the number. In 2008, four-plus players wore

#6—Gustavo Molina, Nick Evans, Abraham Núñez, Trot Nixon, and then Nick Evans again, thus the plus. Perhaps the most beloved player to ever wear #6 was Wally Backman, who donned the number from 1981 to 1988.

METS FIRST-ROUND DRAFT PICKS

LET'S TAKE A SHORT BREAK FROM THE Q&A FORMAT OF THIS BOOK JUST to talk some baseball—specifically first-round draft picks made by the Mets. Earlier, we discussed the Mets' first overall number one pick—Steve Chilcott—and their most recent number one overall pick—Paul Wilson. In all, throughout their history, the Mets have selected first overall in the draft five times—in 1966 (Chilcott), 1968 (Tim Foli), 1980 (Darryl Strawberry), 1984 (Shawn Abner), and 1994 (Wilson). However, the Mets have had many more first-round picks in their history—through the 2022 season, 65 first-round picks to be exact. Some have worked out well, but most—well, not so well.

Of the 65 first-round picks the Mets have made, 25 have been pitchers and 40 have been position players. Let's break things down by decade and see how the Mets have done with their first-round picks. Some of these names you will certainly recognize, while others will have no meaning in your life—or in the history of the Mets franchise—whatsoever.

1960s: With the draft beginning in 1965, the Mets first first-round draft pick was spent on a British-born left-handed pitcher named Les Rohr, who had three ill-fated seasons with the Mets. In 1966, as mentioned earlier, was what best can be described as the Steve Chilcott disaster. The Mets could have had Reggie Jackson, and they chose not to. It is hard to dress that up in any way. In 1967, the Mets drafted left-handed pitcher Jon Matlack, which was their first terrific pick as a franchise. Matlack went on to win the 1972 National League Rookie of the Year Award, was a key part of the 1973 pitching rotation that won the National League pennant, and was the co-MVP of the 1975 All-Star Game. In 1968, the Mets selected Tim Foli first overall, but in 1972 Foli was traded to Montreal as part of a package that saw Rusty Staub come to the Mets. Since Staub on the Mets was a success, it is hard to argue with the Foli pick. It is hard not to argue with their first-round pick in 1969, however. Right-handed pitcher Randy Sterling only spent three games in the majors for the Mets, but it is acceptable to give the Mets a pass on their 1969 pick—after all, they were busy getting ready to shock baseball and the world.

1970s: The Mets had a dubious start to making first-round picks, as their 1970 selection not only decided to turn down the Mets but turned down the majors altogether. Instead of signing with the Mets, shortstop George Ambrow decided to take his talents to college at USC. He never played professional baseball. In 1971, the Mets picked second baseman Rich Puig, who only played in four career major-league games. Tough start to the 1970s for the Mets' front office. Things brightened considerably in 1973, however, when the Mets took Brooklyn's own Lee Mazzilli with their first-round pick. Of course, Mazzilli was a fan favorite, an All-Star, and returned at the end of his career to be a part of the 1986 championship team. In 1974, the Mets selected Cliff Speck, another player who never appeared in the majors for them, but did rack up 13 games in 1986 for the Braves—12 years after being drafted. In 1975 and 1976, the Mets continued their less-than-stellar first-round drafting by selecting catcher Butch Benton and outfielder Tom Thurberg. While Benton had a cup of coffee in the big leagues, Thurberg, who was later converted to a pitcher, never made it out of the minor leagues.

That brings us to 1977, and the Mets best first-round pick by far—an undersized infielder out of Aloha High School in Oregon named Wally Backman. Of course, Backman would end up being one of the grittiest Mets to ever put on the Orange and Blue and played a big role on the 1986 championship team. The following year was also a good one for the Mets in the draft, as they made Hubie Brooks their top pick in 1978. Brooks, who was drafted as an outfielder out of Arizona State University, made a splash with the Mets at third base in the early 1980s, quickly became a fan favorite, and in 1984 tied a team mark with his 24-game hitting streak. Ultimately, Brooks was dealt to Montreal as part of the package the Mets sent to the Expos for All-Star catcher Gary

Carter. However, Brooks did return to the Mets for the 1991 season and actually tied his career high in home runs with the Mets by hitting 16 long balls. That leaves 1979, when the Mets selected Tim Leary with their top pick. Leary enjoyed some success in the majors during a 13-year career, but not with the Mets.

1980s: At the start of the 1980s, the Mets' futility in the latter part of the previous decade began to pay off in terms of the number of first-round draft picks they would have. In 1980, the Mets had three first-round picks—number 1, number 23, and number 24. For the first time in 15 years of making first-round picks, the Mets hit the jackpot with their top pick. Selecting first overall, the Mets chose a teenager out of Crenshaw High School in Los Angeles with a funny last name—Darryl Strawberry. "You could be a black Ted Williams," his college coach Brooks Hurst had told him. To which Strawberry replied, "Who's Ted Williams?" Mets 1983 interim manager Frank Howard was quite confident Strawberry would make his mark with the Mets. "If we miss on this young man, we all better look for a career change." Strawberry, of course, turned into one of the greatest players in franchise history, as Strawberry won the National League Rookie of the Year in 1983, was part of the nucleus in the Mets' 1986 and 1988 teams, and was a seven-time All-Star and two-time Silver Slugger for the Mets. The other two first-round picks for the Mets were not quite as successful as Strawberry, although how could they be. Still, the Mets thought they had hit another jackpot with outfielder Billy Beane. Yes, that Billy Beane. However, Beane's well-documented struggles prevented him from becoming anything with the Mets—although having Brad Pitt portray you in a major film is not a bad accomplishment! The Mets' third first-round pick of 1980 was used to select catcher John Gibbons, who played a handful of games for the Mets in 1984 and 1986. He went on in the 2000s to manage the Toronto Blue Jays for two separate stints.

In 1981, the Mets had just one first-round pick and with that they took an outfielder by the name of Terry Blocker, who played 18 games with the Mets in 1985. The Mets made up for the Blocker pick one year later, however, as they had the fifth pick of the first round in 1982. The Chicago Cubs had the top pick and went with shortstop

Shawon Dunston, who had a very productive career. The second pick went to the Blue Jays, who took someone named Augie Schmidt. The San Diego Padres took a pitcher named Jimmy Jones and the Minnesota Twins took Bryan Oelkers with the fourth pick. Now it was time for the Mets, who were pretty confident with their pick—a very young pitcher by the name of Dwight Gooden. Yes, four other teams passed on Gooden, and the Mets could not have been happier. After Gooden had been drafted by the Mets, one of their roving instructors in the minor leagues, Davey Johnson, had the opportunity to watch Gooden pitch for a few weeks in the rookie-level Appalachian League. "He was the best pitching prospect I ever saw," Johnson recalled. By 1984, Johnson was the manager of the Mets and Gooden was his rookie sensation, winning 17 games and striking out a major-league-best 276 batters. He cruised to the National League Rookie of the Year Award, and the following year his 24-4 record and 1.53 ERA made him the only choice for National League Cy Young Award winner. He won another 17 games in 1986, 15 in 1987, and 18 in 1988. Only off-field troubles were Gooden's nemesis. He did return from a season-ending injury in 1989 to win 19 more games the following year. It is amazing to think about what was, and frustrating to think what could have been.

OK, we are still in the first half of the 1980s, as the Mets had three first-round picks in 1983, none of which turned out anywhere as well as Gooden. With the fourth-overall pick in 1983, the Mets selected a third baseman named Eddie Williams. Among the players the Mets passed on that season was a pitcher at the University of Texas named Roger Clemens, who went 19th overall. Within one year, they had traded Williams to the Cincinnati Reds in exchange for pitcher Bruce Berenyi. With their second pick—the 20th overall and one after Clemens—the Mets took Stan Jefferson, who was traded early on—hang on a minute for that story—and with the 27th overall pick they selected pitcher Calvin Schiraldi, who was traded two seasons later as part of the deal that brought Bob Ojeda to New York. Of course, both Schiraldi and Ojeda played major roles in the 1986 season and postseason for the Red Sox and Mets, respectively.

The Mets had the number one overall first-round pick in 1984 and selected a can't miss phenom by the name of Shawn Abner. Only something happened on the way to Flushing—he missed. Right after selecting Abner, a 17-year-old out of Mechanicsburg High School in Pennsylvania, Mets scouting director Joe McIlvaine raved about his selection. "I have watched Shawn play in the American Legion All-Star game since his sophomore year," McIlvaine told reporters. "He's a big strong kid, physically mature for a 17-year-old. He has quickness, power, runs well—an above average outfielder with a strong arm." Abner was exactly what the Mets—or any major-league team for that matter—needs. Among the players that Abner was selected in front of were Jay Bell and Mark McGwire. Abner never made it higher than Double-A with the Mets, however. He was traded following the 1986 season—along with 1983 pick Stan Jefferson and fan-favorite, but not front-office-favorite Kevin Mitchell—in exchange for Kevin McReynolds. Abner never found his groove in the majors and was out of the game by 1993.

In 1985, the Mets selected a player with their first-round pick who was certainly one of the most complicated players they ever had. Gregg Jefferies burst on the scene for the Mets late in the 1988 season and in 29 games, ripped six home runs, drove in 17 runs, and actually received a few votes on the Rookie of the Year ballot. By 1989, Jefferies was up with the Mets for good, proving he was a very good hitter, capable of leading the National League with 40 doubles in 1990, but also known for being a hothead, who seemed at times to care more about his individual success than team success, and did not really have a position that he fit in perfectly. Following the 1991 season, Jefferies was traded along with McReynolds to the Kansas City Royals for pitcher Bret Saberhagen. Suffice to say that none of this worked out well for the Mets. The remaining picks in the 1980s for the Mets were about as successful as their acquisition of Saberhagen. In 1986 they took Lee May Jr., in 1987 they took Chris Donnels, in 1988 they took Dave Proctor, and in 1989 they took Alan Zinter. Enough said.

1990s: In the early 1990s, the Mets had varying success with their first-round draft picks. In 1990 they selected a young outfielder named Jeromy Burnitz. After spending parts of two seasons with the Mets in the early 1990s, he was traded to Cleveland for a bunch of players who never did much for the Mets, including Paul Byrd, Dave Mlicki, and Jerry DiPoto. Of course, Mlicki did win the first-ever interleague game played at Yankee Stadium, but overall, not a big resume for these guys. Of course, in 2002 Burnitz would return to the Mets and indeed become public enemy number one—at least until Jason Bay got to town. But we digress. In 1991, the Mets took outfielder Al Shirley, who never made it to the majors, and pitcher Bobby Jones, who will appear in a big spot later on in this book, so stay tuned for that. In 1992, the Mets once again had three first-round picks and took Preston Wilson, pitcher Chris Roberts, and pitcher Jon Ward. Neither Roberts nor Ward ever reached the majors. Wilson, however, is another story entirely—with a nice sprinkle of Mets legacy, as he is both the nephew and stepson of Mets great Mookie Wilson. Yes, that is correct—Preston's father was Mookie's brother. Mookie's brother and Preston's mother broke up and Mookie ended up marrying Preston's mother. I don't see why that has to be so complicated. What is quite clear, however, is that Preston Wilson's contribution to the Mets goes beyond whom he is related to, and well beyond the eight games he played for the team in 1998. Preston Wilson, it turns out, was the key to the trade with the Florida Marlins that brought Mike Piazza to the Mets. Preston did make his own mark in the majors, however, spending 10 years for a total of six different teams. His best year was with the Colorado Rockies in 2003, when he hit 36 home runs, 43 doubles, and 141 runs batted in. It is safe to say the Mets were more than satisfied for what they got in return in that trade. In 1993, the Mets selected a pitcher named Kirk Presley who never made it out of the minor leagues. There was an opportunity to have a great pick that year, though, as among the players selected in the first round after Presley were Billy Wagner, Derrek Lee, Chris Carpenter, Torii Hunter, and Jason Varitek.

In 1994, the Mets had the first overall selection in the first round of the draft, and they felt they might have their next ace on the board. Unfortunately, things did not work out that way for the Mets—or for Paul Wilson. Drafted out of Florida State University, Wilson was about as sure a thing as you could get. The headline the next day in the *New York*

Times exclaimed: "Gooden, Seaver, Ryan, and now Wilson?" Of course, it would have been worse if the question mark had been an exclamation mark, but it might as well have been. "Wilson, whose fastball is clocked in the high 90's and who also features a major league caliber slider, was immediately touted as the sort of pitcher with the ability to become a franchise savior as Gooden was," Claire Smith wrote in the *New York Times*. What no one could predict at the time were the injuries that would plague Wilson throughout the early part of his career. After a poor 5-12 start in the majors in 1996, Wilson suffered from a variety of injuries in the next several years and never approached the potential he was touted with and became a journeyman pitcher far too early in his career—especially for someone who was selected with the first overall pick. The Mets had two other picks in 1994, and took Terrence Long 20th and Jay Payton 29th. Of the two, Payton—a top prospect from Georgia Tech—made the biggest impact for the Mets, although he too suffered through a myriad of injuries during his career. Still, Payton was a part of the 1999 and 2000 Mets teams that reached the postseason, starting in center field and helping the Mets make it to the 2000 World Series.

Things did not go well for the Mets in the draft for the remainder of the 1990s, as Ryan Jaroncyk (1995), Robert Stratton (1996), Geoff Goetz (1997), and Jason Tyner (1999) never became household names among Mets fans. It should be noted that Goetz was part of the trade with Florida that brought Mike Piazza to the Mets. As punishment, because of their poor drafting, the Mets did not have a first-round pick in 1999. Well, that is not exactly true, but they were drafting poorly and they did not have a pick in 1999. However, the real reason was that they lost their pick to the Chicago White Sox as compensation for signing free agent third baseman Robin Ventura. So, in essence, they drafted Ventura in 1999—their best pick of the decade by far!

2000s: While through the 1990s, the draft was truly a hit-or-miss proposition for the Mets, things started to change in the 2000s. All of a sudden, first-round draft picks would end up becoming much more important figures in the future of the team. Perhaps—and this has not been mentioned up to this point—the person and people making the picks need to be noted. If the people making many of the picks in the

1980s and 1990s missed the mark, then the people making those picks in the 2000s and beyond should be applauded for doing their jobs well. Remember, the best hitters in baseball fail 7 out of 10 times. Do those making first-round draft picks have that same luxury?

Also worth considering, as the turn of the century rolled into the early 2000s—for whatever reason—there were fewer and fewer good, talented prospects. We know that fewer young athletes are choosing to pursue baseball over the past few decades and that certainly trickles down to the talent pool available in the draft. Enough pontificating, 2000 was a draft that yielded little talent for the major leagues. Of the 30 first-round draft picks in 2000, only three would ever go on to become All-Stars— Adrián González, Chase Utley, and Adam Wainwright. The Mets' picks not only did not become All-Stars, but they never became Mets, as they selected pitchers Billy Traber and Bobby Keppel.

Stop! Breaking News! Well, not really breaking news because it broke a really long time ago, but things changed significantly for the Mets and the draft in 2001. In fact, everyone reading this will actually know all of those picks' names—and how significant they figured into the franchise. In 2001, the Mets had the 18th pick and a supplemental 38th pick, as compensation for pitcher Mike Hampton signing with the Colorado Rockies. With their first pick, they selected Aaron Heilman—who had some very productive years on the mound for the Mets and was a part of the 2006 pitching staff that went all the way to the National League Championship Series. However, Heilman was not the key to the 2001 draft for the Mets, it was that supplemental pick. With the 38th pick, the Mets selected a young third baseman out of Hickory High School in Virginia named David Wright. Not much more has to be spoken about here, as Wright worked out pretty well as a draft pick. If injuries had not derailed his career, we might be writing about his journey to Cooperstown, but that is one of the greatest "what ifs" in Mets history.

In 2002, the Mets selected their next ace—again. However, once again things did not work out the way the Mets had hoped. So began the mysterious saga of Scott Kazmir. After being drafted, the high school star arrived in the organization and quickly established himself as a top prospect throughout baseball. In five starts and 18 innings with the Brooklyn

Cyclones in 2002, the 18-year-old Kazmir struck out 34 batters and allowed only one earned run (0.50 ERA). *Baseball America* ranked him as the 11th best prospect in baseball coming into the 2003 season. The Mets decided to deal with the present rather than the future though, and sent the young fireballer to the Tampa Bay Rays in the summer of 2004 in exchange for Victor Zambrano. Unfortunately for the Mets, nothing came of 2004. Unfortunately for Kazmir, things did not work out so well, either. Although he had flashes of brilliance over his 13-year big-league career, it is hard to picture what might have been if the Mets had experienced just a small amount of that brilliance in the 2000s. Another "what-if." In the following draft, the Mets selected Lastings Milledge—a five-tool player who was about to take the Mets by storm. Milledge had been predicted to be one of the top picks in the draft, but issues away from the field scared many teams off. The fact that he fell all the way to pick number 12, where the Mets grabbed him, should have been a red flag; between the draft and signing with the team, there were allegations of sexual misconduct. After an investigation, the Mets went ahead and signed Milledge, who made his major-league debut in 2006. Controversy always followed Milledge, and by the 2007 offseason the Mets had had enough and traded him to the Washington Nationals. Injuries curtailed what might have been that storm that the Mets had hoped for.

In 2004, the Mets had the number three overall pick—their highest pick since they had selected Paul Wilson first overall 10 years earlier. This time, the Mets once again went with a young right-handed pitcher, Philip Humber. With the pick before Humber, the Detroit Tigers took a pitcher themselves—Justin Verlander, who of course spent half of 2023 with the Mets before being dealt away in the trade-deadline fire sale. Disaster struck before Humber could even start his career when he needed to have Tommy John surgery early in 2005. Once he returned though, the Mets seemed to race Humber to the majors—not from a health point of view, but from an experience point of view, mostly because the pitchers on the major-league roster were dropping like flies. There were so many injuries, in fact, that Humber was forced to start in some high-pressure games that perhaps he was not ready for. Still, he was one of the top prospects in all of baseball in 2007 when the Mets started to talk to the Minnesota

Twins about making a trade for pitching great Johan Santana. Then, just like that, he was gone. Santana became a Met and we all know how that went, and Humber fell into obscurity in Minnesota. He never turned out to be the phenom everyone in the Mets' front office had expected, and by 2012 he was a 29-year-old journeyman pitcher. That is when he had his finest moment, pitching a perfect game as a member of the Chicago White Sox. "You would think to be perfect, you have to be great first. And it's true, the list of perfect game pitchers is mostly Hall of Famers, Cy Young Award winners and multi-year All-Stars," David Adler wrote for MLB.com. "But it also has Humber."

In 2005, the Mets selected a pitcher would play a large role with the team for several years. Mike Pelfrey, for a time, was the Mets' top pitcher on a team desperate for a top pitcher. However, the sum of Pelfrey's parts added up to simply a mediocre career. Just one year after being drafted, Pelfrey reached the majors with the Mets and pitched fine for the team from 2007 through 2009. It was in 2010, however, that he really made a splash. He ended up winning 15 games for the Mets that season, after a 10-1 first half. However, there was much more "fine" than "splash" throughout Pelfrey's career. The following draft the Mets did not have a first-round selection because they signed free agent relief pitcher Billy Wagner.

In the 2007 and 2008 drafts, the Mets had a total of five picks—three of them supplemental selections from other deals, although, for the most part these supplemental picks were much more inconsequential picks. In 2007, Eddie Kunz and Nathan Vineyard were selected, while in 2008, Ike Davis, Reese Havens, and Bradley Holt made the cut for the Mets. Now you might be saying, "Hang on, Ike Davis was a good player." He actually was, for a moment. From 2010 through 2014, the son of former major-league pitcher Ron Davis gave Mets fans some thrilling defense and timely hitting in his first two seasons. Then, in 2012, he broke out—hitting 32 home runs and driving in 90 runs—while playing Gold Glove–caliber defense. In 2013, however, things went south—far south—and Davis hit just .205 with nine homers and 33 RBIs. By April 2014, he was a member of the Pittsburgh Pirates. The Mets did not have a first-round selection in the 2009 draft.

2010s and 2020s: The Mets had success early and often in the draft in these years, beginning with their selection of Matt Harvey seventh overall in the 2010 draft—one of the greatest in recent memory. Not Matt Harvey, but the 2010 draft, which included players such as Bryce Harper, Manny Machado, Jameson Taillon, Yasmani Grandal, Chris Sale, and Christian Yelich. Some of his feats are mentioned elsewhere in these pages, though space does not permit an exhaustive recounting of Harvey's tenure with the Mets. But perhaps no player in Mets history had a rise and fall like Harvey. In 2011, the Mets selected Brandon Nimmo 11th overall. It was not for another decade that the Mets and their fans would understand how important that pick would be, as Nimmo was key in the 101-win season the Mets had in 2022. The Mets had a supplemental first-round pick in the 2011 draft and used it on pitcher Michael Fulmer. Four years later Fulmer, who had never gotten above Double-A for the Mets, was the key player sent to the Detroit Tigers in the trade for Yoenis Céspedes in 2015. The deal seemingly worked out for both sides initially. Céspedes led the Mets to the National League pennant in 2015 and Fulmer won the American League Rookie of the Year Award in 2016 and was an All-Star in 2017. However, just as Céspedes declined, so too did Fulmer. Multiple surgeries led to Fulmer being a shell of what he once was, although he remained with the Tigers until the summer of 2022, when he was dealt to the Minnesota Twins. In 2012, the Mets selected Gavin Cecchini, who had limited time in the majors, and catcher Kevin Plawecki, who served as a Mets catcher for five seasons and has played in Cleveland, Boston, and Texas.

The Mets' 2013 and 2014 first-round picks, Dom Smith and Michael Conforto, appeared for a time to be selections that would benefit the team for years to come. In 2015, Conforto burst on the scene, jumping from Double-A to the majors with much fanfare. Before you blinked, Conforto was playing with the Mets in the World Series and became just the second rookie in World Series history to hit two home runs in a game—which he did in Game 4 against the Kansas City Royals. By 2016, Conforto was the Mets' starting left fielder, but his bat stayed in 2015 and he was sent to the minors. However, Conforto once again found his stroke and was a major part of the Mets through the 2020 season. Prior to the 2021 season the Mets offered Conforto a $100 million contract, which he declined. He went on to have a dreadful 2021 season, batting just .232. At the end of the season, the Mets offered him a one-year, $18 million contract which he declined, instead going into free agency. The work stoppage and an injury conspired against Conforto, who did not play at all in 2022. Dom Smith, on the other hand, had established himself as a key Met, respected for what he did on and off the field. Despite having Pete Alonso at first base, the Mets held on to Smith once it became apparent that the National League would soon be using a designated hitter beginning in 2022. However, Smith failed in the role and in 2022 only hit .194 before finally being demoted to the minor leagues. Also, for whatever reason, he lost the ability to hit home runs, hitting none in his 152 plate appearances for the Mets. He did perform better once he arrived at Triple-A Syracuse, but never made the triumphant return to the Mets that he had been hoping for in 2022. In 2015, the Mets did not have a first-round selection.

It is far too early to really know how the Mets' draft picks from 2016 through 2022 will do, as not enough time has passed. In 2016, the Mets took two pitchers—Justin Dunn and Anthony Kay—who were subsequently traded, and in 2017, they took David Peterson, who was a part of the 2022 season. In 2018, the Mets selected Jarred Kelenic and promptly traded him to Seattle in exchange for Robinson Canó and reliever Edwin Díaz. The Mets were blasted by fans and the media for this trade, as Kelenic's potential was sky high and Canó had seen better days. However, following the 2022 season and the performance by closer Edwin Díaz, the best in all of baseball, talk of the trade being a disaster has subsided. Plus, Kelenic—in parts of two seasons with the Mariners—only hit for an average of .168 and spent much more time in the minors than he did in the majors. As of the end of the 2023 season, Kelenic has hit just 30-something homers in his first three seasons. In 2019, the Mets selected Brett Baty—who, in 2022, homered on the second pitch he saw in the majors. Injuries slowed Baty in 2022, and he seemed to regress a bit in 2023—ultimately being sent to the minors—but he figures to be a key piece in the Mets' future. In 2020 the Mets selected Pete Crow-Armstrong, whom they ended up trading to the Chicago Cubs in July 2021 for Javier Baez and Trevor Williams. In 2021, the Mets selected Kumar Rocker, a pitcher out of Vanderbilt University, but did not sign him due to health concerns. Finally, in 2022 the Mets made two first-round picks—catcher Kevin Parada out of Georgia Tech and shortstop Jett Williams. "I'm elated to be part of the Mets' organization right now," Parada said upon signing. "I'm super excited that they believe in me, and I'm ready for the next steps."

Selecting first-round draft picks is hardly an exact science. The Mets have had some wins, but have suffered more losses—not unlike the rest of their history.

WHO'S (NOT) ON FIRST?

LET'S DO THE MATH HERE—A BOOK ABOUT FIRSTS, IN A SPORT THAT includes a first baseman, combined with a variation on a classic Abbott and Costello routine. That all adds up for some fun. Here is how this will work: For each of the seven decades that the Mets have existed, we will share a list of four players—three of whom played first base at some point for the Mets—one who did not. Your assignment, if you choose to accept it, is to decide who was *not* on first base during the decade in question! If at first, you don't succeed . . .

1960s

1. Ed Kranepool   2. Donn Clendenon   3. J. C. Martin
4. Bud Harrelson

Ed Kranepool, an original Met as a teenager out of New York City, is definitely someone who played first base for the Mets for many years. While Donn Clendenon did not arrive to the Mets until 1969, he is a memorable figure for his play in the 1969 World Series. His position was first base, so he checks out, as well. J. C. Martin only spent two years at the end of the 1960s with the Mets and was a backup catcher for Jerry Grote for most of that time. He did, however, appear at first base in both seasons with the Mets. That leaves, without a doubt, the best fielding infielder of the foursome as the answer, as two-time All-Star and Gold Glove shortstop Bud Harrelson never played first base during his career. He spent all of his time on the left side of the infield at Shea and was regarded as one of the steadiest fielders in franchise history.

1970s

1. Ed Kranepool   2. John Milner   3. Lee Mazzilli
4. Joel Youngblood

As he did in the 1960s, original Met Ed Kranepool spent the entire decade of the 1970s as a member of the Mets, playing first base and pinch-hitting. The rest of the 1970s, for the most part, saw two players— John Milner and Lee Mazzilli—man first base. One player who did not play first base for the Mets, however, is the man who played more different positions than any other player in the decade—and he was only on the Mets for two and a half seasons in the 1970s. Joel Youngblood played second base, shortstop, third base, and all three outfield positions for the Mets from mid-1977 through 1979. Perhaps no one on the Mets roster during the 1970s was more likely to play first base than Youngblood, but it was not to be.

1980s

1. Ed Kranepool   2. Gary Carter   3. Lee Mazzilli
4. Rusty Staub

Ed Kranepool spent a 17-year career with the Mets, from 1962 through 1979. He did not, however, make it to the 1980 season. Much to his chagrin. Kranepool insists that he could have—and should have—remained with the Mets into the 1980s. "The only reason my numbers diminished at the end of my career was because of [manager] Joe Torre and the fact that he stopped playing me," Kranepool said in recent years. "He didn't manage very well with the Mets. He didn't really know what he was doing. But he really shortened my career just due to inactivity. You can rust away." So now that we know that Kranepool did not play first base for the Mets in the 1980s, it begs the question—Gary Carter did? The answer is, he did indeed. In fact, Carter played first base in 24 games during his time with the Mets in an attempt to rest his knees at a time when there was no DH in the National League.

Ed Kranepool was called up to the Mets in 1962 as a 17-year-old kid from the Bronx and played 18 seasons for the team through 1979.
PUBLIC DOMAIN, VIA WIKIMEDIA COMMONS

1990s

**1. Dave Magadan   2. Keith Hernandez   3. Rico Brogna
4. Butch Huskey**

By the time the 1990s rolled around, Dave Magadan was known well by Mets fans despite splitting his time being a backup first baseman and

139

third baseman for his first four seasons with the team. By the late 1980s, injuries to Keith Hernandez gave Magadan more playing time at first base. Throughout the mid-1990s, Rico Brogna and Butch Huskey each spent time manning first base for the Mets. So just who didn't play first base for the Mets from this list? The answer is the former captain himself, as Hernandez never made it to 1990 with the Mets. After suffering through an injury-plagued 1989 season, Hernandez and the Mets parted ways. Hernandez went on to spend one regrettable season in Cleveland, before retiring following the 1990 season.

2000s

**1. Todd Zeile   2. Jason Bay   3. Mike Jacobs
4. Mike Piazza**

Toward the end of his Hall of Fame career, the Mets insisted on experimenting with Mike Piazza. The slugger had lost some of his catching skills and almost all of his throwing skills, and the Mets were trying anything to keep him in the lineup. In 2003, while rehabbing from an injury, Piazza played first base for the first time at Triple-A Norfolk. "I've always prided myself on doing things the right way," Piazza told reporters at the time. "When I started catching, I spent countless hours running to the backstop like a Labrador retriever the first couple of years. If I'm going to play first, I want to do it the right way." When he returned to the majors in 2003, he played one game at first base, and then another 68 at the position in 2004. While Todd Zeile started his career as a catcher, he played the majority of his games for the Mets at first base, as did Mike Jacobs, before he was traded for Carlos Delgado. The one player the Mets could not hide at first base—or anywhere, for that matter—was Jason Bay. Just the mentioning of Bay's name raises the ire of most Mets fans. However, the epic fail of a signing never played first base for the Orange and Blue.

2010s

**1. Daniel Murphy   2. Ike Davis   3. David Wright
4. Lucas Duda**

Everyone knows that David Wright became a fixture at third base midway through the 2004 season and remained there until his body started to break down. For a franchise that was known, comically so, for having a ridiculous number of third basemen throughout their history, Wright's career put a face to the position forever. Wright was a seven-time All-Star, two-time Gold Glove winner, and two-time Silver Slugger. Still, many third basemen—especially as their bodies started to break down—would move to first base at some point, for at least some games. Wright never did. While Daniel Murphy, Ike Davis, and Lucas Duda—all teammates of Wright—spent much of their time at first base, Wright stayed put on the hot corner, never crossing over to the other side of the diamond. Some experts have wondered if Wright might have had a longer career had the Mets moved him to first base at some point. In 2009, writer Dave Meisel wrote on Bleacher Report, "I'm confident that David could learn to play first base well. He is an open-minded, smart, team-first ballplayer. First base is one of the least complex positions to learn on the field." It never happened, although the idea came up again before spring training began in 2017—a season that Wright would end up missing in its entirety due to injury. "Mets manager Terry Collins did not rule out the possibility of Wright taking some reps at first base during camp, as there is uncertainty about Wright's ability to stay at third base for the long term," Matt Ehalt wrote on NJ.com. "Wright has yet to throw since his off-season neck surgery, and his throws have lost zip the past two years. . . . Wright said he's open to doing whatever the team needs him to do to win, and a position change hasn't been approached yet." It would never happen.

2020s

1. Michael Conforto 2. Pete Alonso 3. Dom Smith
4. James McCann

There are two names on this list that absolutely cannot be correct, and there are two answers on this list that are absolutely possible. Michael Conforto was an outfielder for the Mets for seven seasons, during which he played all three outfield positions. James McCann, on the other hand, arrived to the Mets in 2021 to be the everyday catcher—although injuries and lack of production have certainly derailed the "everyday" part of that plan. The big question is, which one of them—at some point—played first base? Once we have that key piece of information, we will know who did not! And the answer is, drumroll—McCann played seven games at first base for the Mets during his first two seasons with the team. Conforto—who missed the entire 2022 season with an injury before moving on to the San Francisco Giants in 2023—never played first base for the Mets.

POSTSEASON FIRSTS

What was the first year the Mets reached the postseason?

From 1962 through 1968, the Mets never had a winning season. In fact, the closest they had come to a winning season was 1968, when the Mets went 73-89. By the time the 1969 season rolled around, the Mets had spent a full season with manager Gil Hodges, and pitchers Tom Seaver and Jerry Koosman had arrived and were ready to make a major impact. Major indeed. The pair of Mets aces combined for 42 victories. The Mets were 27 games better than they had been the year before and not only finished above .500 for the first time, but they won an incredible 100 games. They outlasted the Chicago Cubs, pulling away to win the new National League East by eight games and advanced to the first-ever National League Championship Series. By the time the 1969 regular season was over, the Mets had already stunned the baseball world. However, no one realized how much more there was to come from this group of Amazin' players.

The Mets took part in the first-ever National League Championship Series. What team did they face?

The New York Yankees' biggest rival is the Boston Red Sox—nothing will ever change that. Sure, there are years where there are other teams that pop up and become year-to-year rivals, but nothing will ever trump Yankees–Red Sox. The Mets have never truly had that type of rivalry. In the 1960s when they became a good team it was the Chicago Cubs; in the 1980s, it was the Cubs again, then the Cardinals, then the Pirates, then the Braves, then the Phillies. The Mets have always truly had a revolving door of rivals. However, if you had to pin down one team that is closer to the Mets' all-time rival than any other, it would have to be the Atlanta Braves. Long before the days of Chipper Jones and John Rocker, Tom Glavine and John Smoltz, Freddie Freeman and Ronald Acuña Jr., there was the 1969 National League Championship Series. For the first time in major-league history, in 1969 there was a new playoff format. It was no longer simply going to be the National League champ versus the American League champ to play in the World Series. There were now divisions—and the Mets won the National League East. They would face off against the winners of the National League West in a best-of-five series for the right to play in the World Series. However, it turned out the NL West champs were no match for the Mets, who defeated Henry Aaron, Orlando Cepeda, Phil Niekro, and the rest of the Braves in three straight games. Tom Seaver outpitched Niekro in the opener, and the Mets slugged nine runs for a 9–5 victory in Atlanta. The next afternoon, the Mets brought their bats again in support of starter Ron Taylor and defeated the Braves, 11–6. Finally, in Game 3 and the only NLCS game played at Shea Stadium in 1969, Nolan Ryan earned the victory and the Mets advanced to the Fall Classic to face the unbeatable Baltimore Orioles.

Who hit the first-ever postseason home run for the Mets in 1969?

Despite scoring nine runs in Game 1 against the Atlanta Braves in the NLCS, the Mets did not hit any home runs. That honor would come in Game 2 when Tommie Agee, who blasted 26 home runs during the regular season, faced Braves pitcher Ron Reed in the second inning. After leading off the game one inning earlier with a single, Agee would eventually come around to score the first run of the game on Ed Kranepool's two-out single to right field. Now in the second inning, after pitcher Jerry Koosman drew a one-out walk, Agee promptly blasted a home run to give the Mets a 3–0 lead. They would continue to pile on against the Braves on this day, as Ken Boswell and Cleon Jones would add home runs of their own. However, Agee was the first to go deep in the playoffs for the Mets.

Who hit the first-ever World Series home run for the Mets?

That historic blast came in Game 2 of the 1969 World Series against the Baltimore Orioles. Donn Clendenon, who went on to set a record with three home runs in the Series—a record for a five-game World Series—got things started when the Mets needed him most. The Orioles, who had won 109 games during the regular season and were heavy favorites to win the World Series, took Game 1 against Tom Seaver and the Mets, 4–1. In Game 2, Clendenon led off the top of the fourth in a scoreless game against Baltimore pitcher Dave McNally and sent a home run deep to the opposite field to give the Mets a 1–0 lead. After the Orioles tied the game, 1–1, in the bottom of the seventh inning, the Mets scored a run in the top of the ninth to earn a 2–1 victory. They would not lose another game in 1969.

Who hit the first grand slam in Mets postseason history?

The Mets did not hit a grand slam home run during the postseason in 1969, 1973, 1986, or 1988. No, it would not be until 1999 that they would accomplish that milestone. In Game 1 of the National League Division Series against the Arizona Diamondbacks, the Mets found themselves tied 4–4 in the top of the ninth inning. Earlier in the game, the hottest Met of them all—Edgardo Alfonzo—had hit a home run off of Arizona ace Randy Johnson. By the ninth inning, when Alfonzo stepped up to the plate, Johnson had left the game and Bobby Chouinard was in the game for Arizona. With two outs and the bases loaded, Alfonzo turned on a 3-1 get-me-over fastball from Chouinard and absolutely crushed a home run deep over the foul pole in left field. "Over the last few years, Edgardo Alfonzo has been a fabulous baseball player who has kind of a star quality," Mets manager Bobby Valentine told reporters after the game. "But he's improving. He's gaining confidence, and with confidence you get performances like you saw tonight."

Who was the first team the Mets faced in the 1973 postseason?

Hardly a work of art, the 1973 season was a true rollercoaster for many of the teams in the National League East. In fact, on July 9 the Mets were wallowing in last place, 12½ games behind first place.

"M. Donald Grant, the team's chairman of the board, held a pregame team meeting and at the conclusion of the gathering, Tug [McGraw] jumped up and yelled 'Ya Gotta Believe!'" longtime Mets PR director Jay Horwitz wrote for the Mets Insider Blog. At the time, Horwitz wrote, some of the Mets thought this was going to be a disaster. "A lot of the guys were a little shocked," said Ed Kranepool, who was Tug's roommate at the time. "Some of us thought Tug was mocking Mr. Grant, which he wasn't. It was Tug being his flamboyant self. To make sure I told him to go over to Mr. Grant and say he meant no ill will." It was far from a disaster; it became a rallying cry that endures to this day. In 1973, it propelled the Mets to an 82-79 record, just good enough to finish first in the National League East. Their reward for believing and winning the division—the Big Red Machine. The 1973 version of the Cincinnati Reds won 99 games during the regular season and stormed into the National League Championship Series to take down the Mets. Of course, things didn't work out that way. Despite the Reds taking the first game, the Mets won three of the next four games and won the five-game series, three games to two.

Who was the first person to reach base for the Mets in the bottom of the 10th inning of Game 6 of the 1986 World Series?

Everyone remembers Game 6 of the 1986 World Series. Some can recite the inning batter for batter, some can do it pitch for pitch. Of course, there is not a Mets fan around who doesn't know or remember how the game ends—with a little roller up along first, that somehow, in some way, got under the glove of first baseman Bill Buckner and dribbled into right field. However, there were many things that had to happen in that inning long before Ray Knight raced home with the winning run. So who started the rally for the Mets? Remember, it was a two-out rally, as both Wally Backman and Keith Hernandez hit harmless flyballs to left field and center field, respectively. Two outs, nobody on. The next batter was Gary Carter, who—according to teammate Bob Ojeda—gave off a vibe before approaching the plate. "If you watch the video with Gary walking to the plate, you see that sense of determination," Ojeda told *Newsday*'s Steven Marcus in 2012. "I mean determination! When Gary went up to the plate, there was a determination in his step, in his swing. When Gary strode to that plate, he was not going to make that out. You can see in his face, Gary was like 'No, I'm not making an out. That's not happening.'" Gary was correct. After fouling off the first pitch and taking two balls out of the strike zone, Carter clubbed a line drive single to left field. He made a very big turn around first base, slammed on the brakes, and clapped his hands together. "That was the spark we needed," Ojeda said. "The other guys fed off it, I'll guarantee you that. You saw it in that at-bat that Gary sparked that fabulous comeback."

Who was the first Mets pitcher to hurl a one-hitter in a playoff game?

There are so many pitchers this could be, right? Was it Seaver, Koosman, Gooden, Ojeda, Matlack? In reality, once you hear that this feat happened in a National League Division Series game, all of those names are eliminated as possible choices—none of them ever pitched in an NLDS game. The first year the Mets participated in that round was in 1999, when they faced the Arizona Diamondbacks. But the first one-hitter took place in 2000, when the Mets faced the San Francisco Giants. Not only did the Mets one-hit the Giants, they did so in the clinching game—allowing the Mets to advance to the 2000 National League Championship Series against the St. Louis Cardinals. So who the heck was it? The man who pitched a one-hitter in the fourth and deciding game of the 2000 NLDS was none other than Bobby J. Jones— the Mets' number four starter. Jones had gone 11-6 during the regular season, with a 5.06 ERA. However, there was every chance that Jones would not even be on the Mets' postseason roster. After starting the season 1-3 and scuffling in June, he was optioned to the Mets' Triple-A affiliate in Norfolk. Jones went down to Norfolk, worked on his mechanics, and went 10-3 for the remainder of the season. Still, it was hard to believe—even as it was taking place—that Jones was able to completely shut down the Giants. "It was the best game of his life," ESPN.com wrote in its list of top playoff performances. "The only hit he allowed was a leadoff double to Jeff Kent in the fifth inning. And among his five strikeouts were two against Barry Bonds." The one-hitter set a Mets record for fewest hits allowed in a postseason game, surpassing Jon Matlack's two-hitter in the 1973 NLCS against the Reds.

Who was the first World Series MVP in Mets history?

Mets fans, understandably, are upset about what the Mets did—or did not do at the trade deadline in 2022—to improve a team that seemed destined to play far into October. Instead of going out and making a big splash, general manager Billy Eppler made some moves he felt would shore up an already talented roster. Players such as Darren Ruf and Tyler Naquin did not work out as expected, and the Mets did not end up playing deep into October. One trade deadline move that worked out just a little bit better for the Mets was in June 1969, when the Mets acquired veteran Donn Clendenon, the tall, powerful first baseman from the Montreal Expos. Just six months earlier, the 33-year-old Clendenon had been traded by Montreal to the Houston Astros but refused to report, and the trade was changed. Good thing for the Mets. This time, Clendenon accepted the trade and was an integral part of the Mets' stretch run to take the National League East. However, Clendenon's impact on the Mets was never felt more greatly than in the 1969 World Series. For the Series, Clendenon batted .357, with three home runs and four RBIs. His three home runs set a record for most home runs in a five-game World Series, a record that was matched by Philadelphia's Ryan Howard in 2008. For his efforts, he was named as the 1969 World Series Most Valuable Player. "When Clendenon was lauded as MVP of the '69 Series, he deflected attention from himself," Richard Goldstein wrote in the *New York Times* at the time of Clendenon's death in 2005. "As he put it, 'there is no most valuable player on this team—we've got lots of them.'"

During the 1986 World Series, who was the first Met to have a multi-homer game?

The 1986 World Series could not have gotten off to a worse start for the Mets. After losing the first two games to the Boston Red Sox at Shea Stadium, the Mets traveled to Fenway Park with a sense of desperation. The Mets, led by a leadoff home run by Lenny Dykstra, went on to win Game 3 and get back into the Series. However, it was in Game 4 when

Gary Carter put two home runs over the Green Monster of Fenway Park. With the game scoreless in the top of the fourth inning, Carter blasted a two-run homer off of Al Nipper for his first home run of the World Series. Then in the top of the eighth inning, with the Mets leading 4–0, he homered to even deeper left field off of Boston reliever Steve Crawford. "After waiting 12 years to get into a World Series, Gary Carter is not about to allow a couple of sore knees, a single sore thumb, a 'beat-up' left palm, a dollop of frustration, a soupcon of fatigue, and assorted other maladies and inconveniences—like the Boston Red Sox—to interfere with his good time," Ira Berkow wrote in the *New York Times*. Carter, himself, did not mince words about the importance of the victory. "We all knew we had to win that one," Carter told reporters. "We all knew that nobody comes back from 3–0 in a best-of-seven series. . . . We knew how important the game was. No one had to tell us. This is a great opportunity, being in the World Series. We may never have the opportunity again in our lifetimes." Actually, Carter never would.

Who was the first Mets catcher to tag out two runners on the same play in a playoff game?

One of the strangest plays in the history of the Mets took place in Game 1 of the 2006 National League Division Series between the Los Angeles Dodgers and the Mets. In the top of the second inning, with two runners on base, Dodgers catcher Russell Martin shot a line drive deep to right field that Shawn Green had no chance to get to. He did, however, recover quickly and played the carom off the wall, firing the ball to the cutoff man, who turned and fired to Paul Lo Duca at the plate in hopes of throwing out Jeff Kent. Little did Lo Duca know he was about to hit the jackpot. The ball arrived in plenty of time for the Mets catcher to put a tag down and get Kent. Then, inexplicably—incredulously—J. D. Drew came racing right behind Kent. Lo Duca calmly tagged out the second runner, for your less than routine 9-4-2-2 double play. "It was a terrible blunder that we had to pay for. . . . More times than not, you're going to pay for it. It'll come back to haunt you. That one certainly did," Dodgers manager Grady Little told reporters after the game. "We come from L.A. We know about traffic jams. We certainly had one right there."

Better yet, as sportswriter Thomas Boswell put it, "Los Angeles has grid-lock. This was brain lock."

What was the first time the Mets went to the postseason in two consecutive seasons?

This has actually only happened twice in franchise history, with the most recent time being 2015 and 2016, when the Mets went to the World Series, followed by winning the wild card the following season. However, the first time this happened was in 1999 and 2000. In 1999, the Mets were enjoying their first full season with Mike Piazza in the middle of their lineup. He was an All-Star, a Silver Slugger, and was at times unstoppable. His great offensive year, combined with solid seasons from players such as Edgardo Alfonzo, Robin Ventura, and John Olerud, propelled the Mets to 97 wins. However, that was only enough to tie for the wild card with the Cincinnati Reds, and the two teams had to play a one-game playoff to decide who would reach the playoffs. That was the game that Al Leiter owned and dominated, pitching a two-hit shutout to send the Mets to the National League Division Series against the Arizona Diamondbacks. The Mets advanced past the Diamondbacks in one of the most dramatic moments in franchise history, when . . . never mind, there will be a question about that later. However, as was the case often in the late 1990s and 2000s, the Atlanta Braves stepped in front of the Mets and eventually eliminated them in the National League Championship Series. The following season, Piazza and his crew once again came up big during the regular season, leading the Mets to 94 victories. However, that was one less than those pesky Braves, who won the National League East by one game—leaving the Mets to have to settle for the wild card for the second straight season. Still, they were back in the playoffs—for the second straight year—for the first time ever. This time—thankfully, for Mets fans—there would be no Braves to get in the way; the St. Louis Cardinals handled the Mets' dirty work. While the Mets were disposing of the San Francisco Giants in their National League Division Series, the Cardinals were sweeping past the Braves in the other NLDS. The Mets, without their annual roadblock in the way, went on to defeat the St. Louis Cardinals and advance to the 2000 World Series.

Who did the Mets defeat in the first round of the 2015 playoffs?

The 2015 Mets were not the best team in baseball; however, by the time October rolled around, they were playing the best in the National League. Buoyed by the play of Yoenis Céspedes and hot hitting and pitching, the Mets arrived in the playoffs with something to prove. The first team in front of them was the Los Angeles Dodgers, who won 92 games during the regular season—two more games than the Mets— and won the National League West. After splitting the first four games of the National League Division Series, the Mets and Dodgers faced off in a winner-take-all Game 5 at Dodger Stadium. After the Mets scored in the top of the first inning, Jacob deGrom gave up two runs in the bottom of the first, before settling in to battle through six innings. In the end, the Mets went on to win the game, 3–2, and advance to the National League Championship Series against the Chicago Cubs.

What pitcher got the first win for the Mets in the 2015 NLCS?

In Game 5 of the National League Division Series, the Mets pitched two of their top pitchers—Jacob deGrom and Noah Syndergaard—which meant that neither of them could start the NLCS against the Chicago Cubs. That honor went to the man they called the Dark Knight—who Mets fans were happy was even still around as an option. Matt Harvey, who returned from major surgery after missing the 2014 season, pitched well for the Mets throughout the regular season. Then things got weird. In early September, Harvey and his agent—Scott Boras—decided to announce their great concern about the Mets' plan to let Harvey pitch more than 180 innings during the regular season. Oh, and they added he should not be used at all during the playoffs. This, understandably upset the Mets—and their fans. "I'm the type of person, I never want to put the ball down. Obviously, I hired Scott, my agent, and went with Dr. [James] Andrews as my surgeon because I trusted them to keep my career going and keep me healthy," Harvey told reporters before a start in September. "As far as being out there, being with my teammates and playing, I'm never going to want to stop. . . . Dr. Andrews said his limit was 180." Then, on September 7, Harvey set the record straight. "You've heard about the 180-185 innings cap. That seems to be the number that will allow me to pitch into the postseason. Regardless of those numbers, I hope everyone knows: I have always wanted to play. I have always wanted to pitch every single chance I get. Especially in the playoffs," Harvey wrote to the fans in the magazine, the *Players' Tribune*. "I understand the risks. I am also fully aware of the opportunity the Mets have this postseason. Winning the division and getting to the playoffs is our goal. Once we are there, I will be there." He was. He was there in Game 3 of the NLDS against the Dodgers, and he was there in Game 1 of the NLCS against the Cubs. Harvey pitched 7⅔ innings, gave up two runs on just four hits, and struck out nine batters to give the Mets the first of what would be four straight victories in the NLCS and a ticket to the World Series.

What pitcher did David Wright hit his first career World Series home run against?

As of the end of the 2015 regular season, David Wright had played in more than 1,550 games, had hit 235 home runs, and had played in two playoff rounds in 2006. He had never, however, played in the World Series. After 12 seasons, Wright battled injury after injury during 2015 and only was able to play in 38 games. However, by the time the postseason rolled around, Wright was not about to let anything stop him. He played in every game of the National League Division Series and every game of the National League Championship Series. The Mets, as unlikely as it seemed earlier in the season, had advanced to the World Series against the Kansas City Royals. In Game 1 of the Fall Classic, Wright had two singles in the Mets' 5–4 extra-inning loss. In Game 2, he went 0-for-4 as the Mets fell behind in the World Series two games to none. Game 3, however, would be the Mets' game, and it would be Wright's game. After falling behind 1–0 in the top of the first inning, Mets center fielder Curtis Granderson led off the bottom of the first inning with a single. That brought up Wright, who was about to accomplish his lifelong dream—launching a World Series home run. With Granderson on first, Wright stepped into the batter's box against Kansas City starting pitcher Yordano Ventura. After winning 13 games during the regular season—and surrendering 13 home runs—Ventura started four games in the 2015 postseason and gave up three home runs.

In the bottom of the second inning, Wright crushed a flyball deep to left field that landed well beyond the original 16-foot-high Great Wall of Flushing. "As a kid, I grew up pretending to be in Game 7, facing a 3-2 pitch, and hitting a homer. It wasn't Game 7, but that was playing through my mind the entire time running around the bases," Wright told WFAN. "I don't do this often, but I allowed myself to look around, see the fans and my family and friends, and soak in the moment. As I crossed home plate and went into the dugout, I looked up, and seeing that place rocking to this day sends chills up my spine. I allowed myself to just enjoy the moment."

David Wright hit his first—and only—World Series home run in 2015 against Kansas City's Yordano Ventura.

When was the first time the Mets reached the postseason following their loss in the 2016 wild card round?

The Mets were fully expecting that the shortened COVID season of 2020 would be their best chance in recent years to reach the postseason. Life was strange enough during the global pandemic, so having a baseball season of just 60 games didn't seem all that strange. The Mets had built a much better team in 2019, led by a hulking rookie who hit a major-league record 53 home runs. Alonso certainly did his part in 2020, as did Robinson Canó and Dom Smith, but the Mets lost their way—and lost a lot of games. There were no playoffs for the Mets in 2020. The Mets would not reach the postseason until 2022, when they won 101 games during the regular season, but fell one game short of the Atlanta Braves for the National League East division title and had to settle for the wild card. Alonso hit 40 home runs and drove in a franchise-record and major-league best 131 runs, and Francisco Lindor hit 26 homers and drove in a career-best 106 runs. The clincher came on September 19, when the Mets defeated the Milwaukee Brewers, thanks to yes—an Alonso home run. In the win, Max Scherzer returned from the injured list and pitched six perfect innings to earn his 200th career victory.

When was the first time the Mets walked off a playoff series?

Late in the 1999 season, the Mets traveled to Philadelphia for an important three-game series. They had just been swept by the Braves in Atlanta. The Mets were in a race with the Cincinnati Reds for the National League wild card. On the day the Mets arrived in Philadelphia, they were one game ahead of the Reds. On the day they left, they were one game behind the Reds. However, being swept by the Phillies, or having the Reds pass them in the wild card standings, wasn't the most important thing that happened that weekend. Instead, it was Mike Piazza getting hit with a backswing—excerbating a summer's worth of injuries. As it would turn out, it was the best thing that could have happened to the Mets. Fast forward to the 1999 National League Division Series against the Arizona Diamondbacks. After going 2-for-9 in the first two games, Piazza's hand was bothering him to the point where he needed a cortisone shot after Game 2. "He woke the next day to find his thumb had swollen to cartoonish proportions, the result of an allergic reaction," Matthew Callan wrote on SBNation. "The swelling should go down in 48-72 hours, he was told. It was cold comfort for him or his team, who would have to play their first home playoff game in 11 years without him. During pregame player introductions, he greeted the crowd in a jacket, his entire left hand wrapped like a mummy." Even without Piazza, the Mets managed to win Game 3 by a score of 9–2. Piazza's replacement, Todd Pratt, went 0-for-2. "To lose your biggest bat in the middle of a playoff series should have been a disaster for the Mets, but they'd already weathered a few disasters that season. Game three turned out to be their most drama-free game of October, as the team accumulated an early lead and allowed the opposition few chances at a comeback," Callan wrote. In Game 4, the Mets and the Diamondbacks headed to the 10th inning with Arizona's backs against the wall. After John Franco set the D-Backs down in order in the top of the 10th, Arizona's Matt Mantei came in to try to hold off the Mets. After Robin Ventura flew out to right field for the first out of the inning, Piazza's replacement—Todd Pratt—came to the plate. He sent a deep flyball to center field that drove Steve Finley back to the wall until his back was up against the fence. As he jumped, the 55,000-plus at Shea Stadium fell silent. Did Finley catch the ball? "Oh, that's hit well to center field," broadcaster Chris Berman said. "Finley goes back, back, back!" Pratt recalled after the game: "Right off the bat, I thought it had enough but then I saw Finley going back—like I've seen him do multiple times—and when he jumped I was like, 'Ah, he got it.' But as soon as he looked down at his glove, I knew he didn't, and the rest is history." The Mets won the game, the series, and advanced to the 1999 National League Championship Series.

Who was the first Mets player to greet Ray Knight at home plate as he got mobbed after scoring the winning run in Game 6 of the 1986 World Series?

As Ray Knight rounded third base and headed toward the plate with the winning run, third base coach Bud Harrelson nearly beat Knight to the plate. "Knight came racing to third base and I not only waved him home, I accompanied him on his journey," Harrelson wrote in his book, *Turning Two*. "I had to slow down because I had Ray beat and I couldn't touch home plate or get there before he did." If he had been a little faster, or if Knight had slowed down at all, Harrelson would have been the first person to embrace Knight. As it was, he was the first person to hug the Mets' third baseman from behind. However, the first teammate to greet Knight was the on-deck hitter, Howard Johnson. It's a little ironic, being that the following season, Knight would be gone and HoJo would be the Mets' third baseman, but at this moment, it was two teammates enjoying one of the greatest moments on a baseball field. No one in the world had a better vantage point for what unfolded than Johnson. "I remember it very clearly," Johnson said three decades later. "Shea had a tough infield. The dirt could be bad at times, and it was late in the game and it was kind of chewed up. I saw the ball hit, and because he got jammed it wasn't hit very hard. But it was bouncing funny, and when Buckner went to get the ball, he was kind of on his heels and never really got in into the right position. He was decidedly not aggressive on that ground ball. When it got to him, you could just see that in-between hop get underneath his glove." Johnson quickly lurched his head to his left—from looking at the groundball to picking up Knight rounding third base—while jumping into the air in celebration. By the time Knight got to the plate, Johnson was there to offer him the first of what would be many bear hugs on that cold October night.

In which game did Tom Seaver get his first World Series win in 1969?

The Baltimore Orioles headed into the 1969 World Series against the Mets with a lot of confidence. They had won 109 games during the regular season, and there was little reason to think these Miracle Mets would be able to defeat this team built on exceptional starting pitching, veteran power bats, and some of the best fielders who had ever lived. Of course, the Mets sent their best pitcher to the mound in Game 1 of the World Series—25-game-winner Tom Seaver. However, the Orioles were not intimidated and countered with 23-game-winner Mike Cuellar. Seaver gave up one run in the first inning and three more in the fourth, which was more than enough for the American League champions, who took the opener, 4–1. The Mets would take the next two games, and

Seaver was tapped to pitch in Game 4. This time, the greatest of them all would not be denied. Seaver pitched all 10 innings of the Mets 2–1 victory, giving up just six hits along the way. The only run Seaver allowed was a sacrifice fly by Brooks Robinson in the top of the ninth inning, to tie the game, 1–1. Of course, this was not just any sacrifice fly—it is the ball on which right fielder Ron Swoboda made one of the most incredible catches in World Series history. In the top of the 10th inning, Seaver worked around an error and a single and stranded two runners on base. In the bottom of the 10th, with pinch-runner Rod Gaspar on second base and Al Weis on first, the Mets' J. C. Martin put down a sacrifice bunt. Baltimore pitcher Pete Richert—who had just entered the game—hit Martin with the throw and it bounced away, allowing Gaspar to race home with the winning run. Seaver's 10 innings, plus a dash of Swoboda magic, made for the first World Series win for the ace. "Swoboda's sprawling dive in shallow right-center on Brooks Robinson's sinking fly ball meant the Orioles only tied the game instead of surging ahead, and New York went on to win the game in extra innings to seize firm control of the series," Tim Britton wrote years later in *The Athletic*.

Who was the first Mets pitcher to get a base hit in a playoff game?

This question could have been asked in an even more aggressive way, but the thought of asking, "who was the first Mets *relief* pitcher to get a base hit in a playoff game?" seemed a little extreme. So did, "who was the first Mets relief pitcher to get *two* hits in a playoff game?" The answer is the same to all three versions of the question. On the day of Gary Gentry's 23rd birthday, manager Gil Hodges handed him the ball for Game 3 of the 1969 National League Championship Series against the Atlanta Braves. The Mets were already leading the best-of-five series and were hoping that the birthday boy could lock down the clincher. He could not. After Gentry pitched 2⅓ innings, during which he gave up two runs, five hits, a home run, and a walk, Hodges had seen enough. He went to the bullpen with one out in the top of the third inning and brought in the young fireballer, Nolan Ryan, who was fantastic. Ryan pitched for 6⅔ innings, gave up two runs on three hits, and struck out seven batters. He also had a successful day at the plate. In the bottom of the fifth inning, Ryan singled to right field off of Atlanta's Pat Jarvis. He came in to score two batters later when Wayne Garrett homered. In the bottom of the eighth inning, Ryan stood in the batter's box for the fourth time of the game—and promptly laced a single to center field. For his career, which spanned a total of 27 years, he had just a .110 lifetime batting average.

What pitcher earned the first win of the 2015 World Series for the Mets?

After losing the first two games of the 2015 World Series in Kansas City, the Mets knew that Game 3 at Citi Field was a must-win. It was the first World Series game ever to be played at the stadium that opened in 2009, and the Mets sent fan-favorite—at the time—Noah Syndergaard to the mound. The man they called Thor was not happy apparently with the way his teammates had been treated in Kansas City and had vowed to send a message to the Royals. He did exactly that with his very first pitch—a fastball over the head of leadoff hitter Alcides Escobar. "The 98-mph fastball went whizzing over his head, buckling him, leaving his legs straddling home plate, and staring at Syndergaard in disbelief," Bob Nightengale wrote for *USA Today*. "He never even moved until Mets catcher Travis d'Arnaud motioned him to get up." The Royals bench erupted. After the game, the Mets pitcher did not back down at all. "If they have a problem with me throwing inside," Syndergaard told reporters, "then they can meet me 60-feet, six-inches away. I've got no problem with that." In Game 3, the Royals had problems with Syndergaard, period, as the Mets pitcher allowed just three runs over six innings in the 9–3 Mets victory. Syndergaard didn't deny his first pitch was intentional, nor did he apologize for it. However, the Royals would have the last laugh in the World Series. On this night, however, Syndergaard earned the win, making him the first pitcher to win a World Series game at Citi Field.

Who hit the first postseason home run at Citi Field for the Mets?

We all know the year—2015, the first time the Mets had reached the playoffs since winning the National League East in 2006. However, in

2006 the Mets were still playing at Big Shea. Since the Mets had moved into Citi Field, they had not really sniffed the postseason. Yet here they were, in Game 3 of the National League Division Series against the Los Angeles Dodgers. The Mets and Dodgers had split the first two games at Dodger Stadium, and this game would prove to be a big one for the Mets. The bats exploded to score 13 runs on 13 hits, but only two of those hits would be home runs. The first of the game—and the first in the history of Citi Field postseason play—came in the bottom of the fourth inning when catcher Travis d'Arnaud blasted a two-out, two-run homer to left. Travis had himself a night in Game 3, going 3-for-5, with three RBIs and three runs scored. This seemed unlikely heading into the game, as d'Arnaud had been struggling at the plate—0-for-7, with four strikeouts in the NLDS. "Today I was just trying to keep things simple," d'Arnaud told reporters after the game. "I feel like, the last few weeks, I've been overthinking and trying to do too much instead of just seeing the ball and hitting the ball."

When did Mike Piazza hit his first postseason home run for the Mets?

As discussed earlier, Mike Piazza was hurting during the 1999 postseason. A season's worth of foul tips, backswings, crouches, and the like had beaten down the big guy by the time the playoffs came around. It was his replacement, Todd Pratt, who hit the walkoff home run against Arizona to send the Mets to the National League Championship Series against the rival Atlanta Braves. However, that series is where Piazza would hit his first postseason homerun for the Mets. Piazza had been a nonfactor for the entire series, going 3-for-20 through the first five games. In Game 6, with their backs against the wall, the Mets fought and clawed their way through the game that started with the Mets allowing five runs to the Braves in the bottom of the first inning. Heading to the top of the seventh inning, the Mets were trailing the Braves 7–3 and being eliminated was becoming more of a reality for New York. It did not make things easier that future Hall of Famer John Smoltz came in to pitch in the seventh for Atlanta. However, the Mets' bats came to life, starting with back-to-back doubles by Matt Franco and Rickey Henderson, to bring the Mets a little closer. After Edgardo Alfonzo flew out to right field, John Olerud drove in Henderson with a single to make it a 7–5 game. That is when Piazza stepped to the plate—and looking for a hit, let alone his first postseason homer as a member of the Mets. He got both in one swing—blasting a Smoltz pitch to the opposite field in right-center and sending it five rows past the 390-mark. "Tied at seven, hoping for Game 7," said broadcaster Bob Costas as Piazza crossed home plate. Unfortunately, there would be no Game 7, as the Braves drew a bases-loaded walk in the bottom of the 11th inning to advance to the World Series.

Who was the first Mets pitcher to win three games during a playoff series?

One of the most underrated postseason series in Mets history is the 1986 National League Championship Series against the Houston Astros. There was no shortage of drama—or animosity—in that series, as the two teams clearly didn't like each other. There was much suspicion that Astros ace Mike Scott—who had earlier in his career pitched for the Mets in a far less ace-like fashion—was scuffing the baseball in some manner. Scott had gone 18-10 in 1986, pitched a no-hitter to clinch the National League West title for the Astros, and won the Cy Young Award. In Game 1, Scott held the Mets to just five hits and defeated his former team, 1–0. The Mets took the next two games, though, thanks to wins by Bob Ojeda—who had 18 himself during the regular season—and reliever Jesse Orosco, who pitched the final two innings of Game 3, giving up no runs on just one base hit. In Game 4, *you know who* got the win for the Astros, holding the Mets to just one run on three hits. To say Scott was in the heads of the Mets would be an understatement. Fortunately for the Mets, they would not see him again in 1986. Game 5 was one of the most memorable playoff games in the history of the Mets, as the starting pitchers were two greats—Nolan Ryan, another former Met— and Dwight Gooden. After Ryan battled for nine innings and Gooden battled for 10, each ended up giving up just a single run. The game would be decided by either Astros reliever Charlie Kerfeld, or Orosco, with a little Gary Carter mixed in for good measure. It was Carter's base hit against Kerfeld in the bottom of the 12th inning that finally clinched the

2–1 win for the Mets. Orosco's two perfect innings of relief earned him his second win of the series. The stage was now set for what would be the craziest, most exciting, heart-pounding game of the NLCS—Game 6. Had it not been for another Game 6 the following week, *this* would be the Game 6 that everyone remembers. The players remember it, for sure. The game went back and forth for 16 innings. When Orosco struck out Houston's Kevin Bass to end the game and send the Mets to the World Series, the lefty became the first Mets pitcher in history to win three games in a postseason series. However, the Game 6 win might have not ever happened had it not been for a pointed conversation between Mets veteran stars Keith Hernandez and Gary Carter. After the Astros scored twice in the bottom of the 16th inning to cut the Mets' lead to 7–5, there was a meeting on the mound that had dual purposes. It was to calm Orosco down, and it also gave Hernandez the opportunity to tell Carter that he felt Orosco was throwing too many fastballs. "I said, 'Kid, if you call another fastball, I'm going to come to home plate and we're going to have to fight,'" Hernandez reported. "Kid told me: 'We're not going to fight.'" Orosco threw nothing but breaking balls for the rest of the inning; he got an out, gave up a single to Glenn Davis to make it 7–6, and finally struck out Bass to end it. No fight needed, and—more importantly—no Game 7 against Mike Scott needed. "He watched from the dugout, he haunted us," Carter told reporters. "He stuck in the back of our minds. No, sir, we didn't want to face him the following day for all the marbles. . . . The man had a power over us even when he was spending the game on the bench." Still, as time passed Carter seemed less haunted. In 2009, Carter was managing the Long Island Ducks—an independent team—and was writing a blog for *Newsday*. "I have often been asked if I thought we could have beaten the Astros in Game 7 back in '86," Carter wrote. "Knowing Scott was looming for a Game 7 was big, and having to face him might have written a completely different story. He was dominant in the other two games we faced him, but knowing our team's character, we would have found a way to win." Fortunately, thanks to Orosco's three series wins, it never came to that.

Which Mets postseason game caused the first-ever cancellation of an episode of Saturday Night Live?

Bill Buckner even ruined *Saturday Night Live*! After 12 straight years of shows, dating back to 1975, *SNL* had never had to cancel an episode—ever. Until the night of Game 6 of the 1986 World Series, that is. The game started, as scheduled, at 8:30 p.m. ET, allowing that the show would start a few minutes late if the game went a normal three-plus hours. However, it went four hours and two minutes, ending at 12:32 a.m., more than an hour after *SNL* was supposed to start. The NBC Television Network decided against airing the show live and instead recorded it for the studio audience beginning at 1:30 a.m. It was aired two weeks later, on November 8, complete with a comedic apology from Mets pitcher Ron Darling. "When we found out that *Saturday Night Live* had been pre-empted, the mood in the locker room dropped quicker than a Roger McDowell sinker ball. Sure, we tried to keep up a front, pretending to be happy after we won the Series, but all we could think about were those disappointed *Saturday Night Live* fans. Even the tickertape parade seemed like a hollow charade. So, on behalf of all the Mets, I would like to make a public apology. We didn't mean to do it, it's just that when you're playing in the World Series, sometimes you get all wrapped up in it, and, well, you forget about what's really important. Believe me, I'd gladly give back my World Series ring if it'd bring the show back live, but it won't, so I'm keeping it," Darling joked.

Who was the first manager to have managed the Mets, and then gone on to win a world championship with another team?

The Mets have had 23 managers in their 60-plus year history and none won more championships than their very first. Yes, the Ol' Professor himself, the most grandfatherly manager of all time—Casey Stengel, who won seven championships as the manager of the New York Yankees. However, that was not the question. Dallas Green, who managed the Mets from 1993 through 1996, also managed a team to a world championship in 1980—when he took the Philadelphia Phillies to the promised land. Again, that was not the question. The question, is who was the first manager to have managed the Mets, and then gone on to win a world championship with another team? It might also have mentioned that it was this manager's first managerial job. Also, the team he won with was not just "another" team. Joe Torre, who managed the Mets from 1977 through 1981, went on to manage the Atlanta Braves from 1982 through 1984, and the St. Louis Cardinals from 1990 through mid-1995. His managerial record up until that point was 894 wins and 1,003 losses. That might be why on the day after he was hired by George Steinbrenner to manage the Yankees, the front page of the *New York Daily News* read, in 120-point type—"CLUELESS JOE"—with the subhead touting, "Torre has no idea what he's getting into." Except, he actually did. "George Steinbrenner wants to win, I want to win, he's the boss, there's no question in my mind," Torre said that day. So, Clueless Joe started to win, and win, and win. In his first eight seasons as Yankees manager, Torre won four championships and two more American League pennants. Of course, one of those championships came at the expense of the first team that gave him the opportunity to manage in the first place.

WHO IS IN YOUR FIRST-STRING METS LINEUP?

OK, WE HAVE BEEN THROUGH A LOT TOGETHER IN TERMS OF METS firsts. We have discussed dozens and dozens of firsts—each holding a special place in Mets history. No matter how many questions you got right, or how many you didn't get right—this is an opportunity for you to be in charge of your own destiny. It is time for you to select your ultimate first-string Mets team. There are no right or wrong answers here, but as you will see, there are a lot of interchangeable parts and countless versions of what can be a first team.

Your version of the best Mets team may not be the same as anyone else's, and that is just fine. Just remember, you can only pick one player at each position, and it must be one of the players offered. No write-in votes. As an extra challenge, and to make your team even more unique, after selecting your squad—construct a batting order. Now you have your first-string Mets team, and the lineup to take on any other fictional team you'd like. First things first, though—select your team!

FIRST BASE (select one)

- **Keith Hernandez:** One of the greatest hitters in team history, batting .297 in his seven years in New York. He won six straight Gold Gloves with the Mets, went to four straight All-Star Games, and won a Silver Slugger Award. He is regarded by most as the greatest fielding first baseman of all time.

- **Pete Alonso:** Alonso burst on the scene as a rookie in 2019 and promptly blasted a major-league rookie record and franchise record 53 home runs. He received 29 of 30 first-place votes and was easily named as the National League Rookie of the Year. In 2022, he hit 40 home runs and led the majors with 131 runs batted in. He hit more than 185 total homers in his five seasons, one of which was the COVID-shortened 2020 campaign.

- **John Olerud:** One of the greatest hitters of his generation, Olerud never took a day off—literally in some cases. In his three years with the Mets he played in 154, 160, and 162 games. In 1998, when he played in 160 games, he finished the season with a batting average of .354, hit 22 home runs, had 36 doubles, and 93 runs batted in. While he never won a Gold Glove with the Mets, he did win three times during his career.

SECOND BASE (select one)

- **Félix Millán:** Not many players in the history of the Mets—or the major leagues, for that matter—were steadier than Millán. The man with perhaps the most impressive mustache of the 1970s played in all 162 games of the season twice in his career, once with the Braves and once with the Mets. In 1975, the year he played every single day, Millán had 191 hits for the Mets. His fielding percentage with the Mets, meanwhile, was nearly .980. Don't sleep on defense when building your perfect lineup!

- **Jeff McNeil:** In 2022, McNeil added something pretty darn impressive to his resume, when he not only won the National League batting title, but was the best in all of Major League Baseball with his .326 average. The two-time All-Star also had an impressive 39 doubles that season.

- **Edgardo Alfonzo:** No player in the history of the Mets was more underrated than Alfonzo. He did spend more time at third base than at second base, but for this exercise we have made him a second baseman. He made only one All-Star team and won only one Silver Slugger Award, but his value was incredible. He hit key homers, got clutch hits, and was—for a time in 1999 and 2000— the best all-around baseball player in New York (and that includes a guy across town who wore #2). In one of his finest moments, Alfonzo went 6-for-6, with six RBIs against the Houston Astros.

THIRD BASE (select one)

- **Howard Johnson:** If you think this is an easy decision, think again. HoJo was Mr. 30-30—three times! Let's put that in perspective, Johnson had more than 30 home runs and 30 stolen bases in the same season three separate seasons. That has only been accomplished by the father-son combo of Bobby and Barry Bonds. In his nine years with the Mets, Johnson hit 191 home runs and stole 202 bases, and played a solid third base. He was a two-time All-Star and two-time Silver Slugger.

- **David Wright:** If you think this is an easy decision, think again. Wright was known as Captain America, but most importantly for the Mets, he was their captain. Wright's numbers in a condensed amount of time are staggering and very underrated. Because of the ways that injuries cut Wright's career short, fans may forget just how great a hitter he was. Here is a reminder: from 2005 to 2010, Wright averaged a .306 batting average, 25 home runs, 40 doubles, 85 RBIs (but he had more than 100 RBIs in five of the six seasons), and 22 steals. On top of that he was a seven-time All-Star, won two Gold Gloves, and two Silver Sluggers.

- **Robin Ventura.** There is no really great third option here, despite the fact that the Mets have had 182 third basemen in their history—through the 2022 season. Of course, the fact that the Mets have had so many speaks to why it is hard to pick a really good third choice. We will go with Ventura, who was a Met for only three seasons, but stood out in 1999, when he hit .301, with 32 homers, and finished sixth in National League MVP voting. Of course, no moment was bigger and more well-remembered from Ventura than his grand-slam "single" to win Game 5 of the NLCS over the Braves.

SHORTSTOP (select one)

- **Francisco Lindor:** The first of three solid choices at shortstop, Lindor won over the Mets fans in 2022 when he had a career year—one season after not doing so at all. Arriving in New York in 2021—and signing a 10-year, multi-hundred-million-dollar extension—there was a lot of pressure for Lindor to produce right away. He did not do so. The career .285 hitter, who had been known for hitting 30-plus homers each season, struggled to hit just .230 with 20 home runs in 2021. However, 2022 was a completely different story, as Lindor bounced back to bat .270, hit 26 home runs, and drive in 107 runs—a franchise best for a shortstop. He also played flawless defense and won over the New York fans. He had an up-and-down 2023 season, but still hit more than 25 homers and drove in more than 80 runs. The best thing that a Mets fan can think about Lindor is "Stay tuned!"

- **José Reyes:** No Mets player has ever burst on the team with more electricity than Reyes. From the day he arrived, there was fast, faster, Reyes! In 2005 and 2006, he led the league in triples and stolen bases. In 2008, he led the league in hits (204) and triples (19). In 2011, he was the batting champion of the National League. A blur as he rounded the bases, a ball in the gap at Shea Stadium meant Reyes was going to leg out a triple. His fielding was always solid, with flashes of brilliance, and he had a smile that never ended. He returned to the Mets at the end of his career and in 2017 had one of his best seasons in years.

- **Bud Harrelson:** There is not a single stat that is going to make you feel that Harrelson should be your pick at shortstop. However, he played in a different era, an era where shortstops had good gloves, no bat, and were true leaders. Harrelson anchored the Mets' infield for 13 seasons, helping to guide them to one world championship and another National League pennant. He did win a Gold Glove in 1971 and, as he likes to put it "hit Pete Rose's fist with his face" in a famous brawl during the 1973 National League Championship Series. No one should ever sleep on Buddy.

CATCHER (select one)

• **Gary Carter:** Always referred to as the "final piece of the puzzle" for the 1986 championship team, Carter was a Hall of Famer before he even arrived in New York. However, when he did arrive in New York, he certainly made the most of it—on and off the field. In his first two seasons with the Mets, the veteran catcher led a young, talented pitching staff of Gooden, Darling, Fernandez, Cone, and others, and managed to average nearly 30 homers and 102 RBIs. Carter was an All-Star in his first four seasons with the Mets and a Silver Slugger in his first two playing at Shea. He was named co-captain of the Mets in 1988.

• **Mike Piazza:** The greatest-hitting catcher of all time arrived in New York to try to replicate the dominance he had with the Los Angeles Dodgers. While in New York, Piazza never matched the batting average numbers he had on the left coast, he quickly became one of the greatest hitters to ever put on a Mets uniform. From 1999 through 2002, Piazza averaged 37 home runs per season, 107 runs batted in, was a four-time All-Star, and a four-time Silver Slugger. He also led the Mets to the playoffs in back-to-back seasons for the first time in their history in 1999 and 2000. Piazza is only the second player to ever enter the Hall of Fame in Cooperstown wearing a Mets cap, and the team retired his #31 soon after.

• **Jerry Grote:** Seaver, Koosman, Gentry, Matlack—all legendary pitchers for the Mets in the late 1960s and early 1970s. However, they needed an equally good catcher to be calling their games, and that man was Jerry Grote. As hard-nosed as a catcher could be, Grote was a defensive specialist, not contributing all that much offensively. He had an all-time fielding percentage of .991 in his

12 years with the Mets and in his best seasons gunned down nearly 50 percent of runners attempting to steal against him.

OUTFIELDERS (select three)

- **Carlos Beltrán:** Beltrán was an underrated Met. Part of the reason for this is that he had a very complicated relationship with the fans. On the field, he would at times be electric, but at other times appeared to be brooding and disengaged. Some of his home runs were simply epic, and he played an incredible center field while a member of the Mets, winning three straight Gold Gloves and averaging 34 homers per year from 2006 to 2008. However, all of the good times seem to be drowned out by the few bad times, including the Adam Wainwright pitch that still has Beltrán's knees buckling. The truth is complex for Beltrán's time with the Mets. What is definitely true, however, is that he was one of the greatest players of his time.

- **Darryl Strawberry:** In the summer of 1983, it quickly became apparent that the tall, slender kid from the rough part of Los Angeles was going to be a special player. Strawberry won the National League Rookie of the Year for the Mets with 26 home runs and 74 RBIs. Compared to Alonso's 53 home runs, the 26 does not seem all that impressive, but in 1983 it was more than impressive, it was flat-out terrific. Strawberry went on to have an exceptional offensive career for the Mets, never having a down year during his eight full years in New York. His power numbers were capped off in 1988 and 1989 when he hit 39 home runs in each season and drove in more than 100 runs. Perhaps his greatest season though was 1987, when he batted .284, hit 39 homers, drove in 104 runs, and stole 36 bases, joining Howard Johnson that year as the first two Mets in the 30-30 Club.

- **Cleon Jones:** When the Mets shocked the Baltimore Orioles— and the world—in 1969, the final out of the game was a flyball off Davey Johnson's bat that settled nicely into Cleon Jones's mitt in left field. Jones batted .340 for the Miracle Mets during the regular season when they would win a franchise-record 100 games. In the 1969 National League Championship Series against the Atlanta Braves, the first-ever playoff series, Jones batted .429, with a home run and four RBIs in the Mets' three-game sweep that landed them in the Fall Classic.

- **Yoenis Céspedes:** Céspedes's last couple of years with the Mets were not good at all. But that first year? Man, that was a doozy. With the full understanding that baseball is a team sport, no man meant more to any team in recent memory as Céspedes meant to the Mets when he was acquired at the trading deadline in 2015. In the final 57 games of the regular season, Céspedes put the Mets on his back and literally carried them to the postseason. He hit 17 home runs and drove in 44 runs in the 57 games and came up with clutch hit after clutch hit. Céspedes immediately became a folk hero who helped the Mets make it to the unlikeliest of World Series. Following the 2015 season, Céspedes had another strong year for the Mets in 2016, leading the Mets to take one of the National League wild cards. After that, not so much, but for two seasons, Céspedes was legendary.

- **Mookie Wilson:** Wilson did not have the power or abilities of many others on this list, but what he did have is flat-out speed—on the bases and in the field. From 1982 to 1984, Wilson averaged more than 50 stolen bases per season and from day one was a fan favorite. Watching him run the bases was about as exciting as it got in the 1980s, and Mookie always—always—had a smile on his face. He also once hit a little roller toward first.

- **Tommie Agee:** In 1969, the Mets found a star in Tommie Agee. After plodding through his first season with the Mets in 1968, Agee found his power, found his confidence, and stroked 26 home runs for the Amazin' Mets. During the regular season in 1969, he became the first man—and only man—to ever hit a fair ball home run into the upper deck at Shea Stadium. To commemorate the home run, there was a round sign painted in Section 48 of the upper deck that included Agee's name, uniform number, and the date—April 10, 1969.

STARTING PITCHERS (Select two)

Special note about this category: There is absolutely no way that any sane person could easily narrow this down to just two starting pitchers, but that's part of the fun of it. Unlike the other positions in this exercise—rather than give a summary of the pitcher's career with the Mets—you will read about their best season, the statistics from that season, and perhaps that, if anything, can help you make your choices. Choose wisely and yes, you can only pick two.

- **Tom Seaver:** How do you pick one of Tom Seaver's seasons and separate it from his overall brilliance? Consider this: Seaver won the Rookie of the Year Award, three Cy Young Awards, was an All-Star pretty much every season he put on a uniform, and is known as "The Franchise." Oh, and he has a statue of his likeness in front of Citi Field. Do we even need to list this guy's best season with the Mets? Flip a coin! Snobbery aside, in 1969—while leading the Mets to the most unlikely baseball season of all time—Seaver went 25-7, with a 2.21 earned run average, struck out 200 batters, completed 18 games, and finished second in MVP voting. So there you go, Seaver's best year. Unless you like one of the others better, I am pretty sure he is making your rotation!

- **Jerry Koosman:** They always say that if Seaver was number one, then Koosman was 1-A, because he was much more than a number two starter for the Mets during his 12-year tenure in New York. Koosman was a master on the mound, and was one of the most respected arms in all of baseball throughout the 1960s and 1970s. Perhaps his best season was his first full season in 1968, when he went 19-12, with a 2.08 ERA and completed 17 games. Oh, he is also one of only two lefty starters on this list.

- **Jacob deGrom:** One thing you cannot do with deGrom is judge him on the number of wins he had in any given season. While the number of wins meant everything in the days of Seaver and

Koosman—and even Viola and Cone for that matter—deGrom's pitching transcended wins. Getting little or no run support for years, yes years, the man they affectionately called deGoat posted miniscule ERAs and ridiculous strikeout-to-walk numbers. Along the way, he won a Rookie of the Year and two Cy Young Awards. His best season had to be 2018, the year of his first Cy Young, when he posted an earned run average of 1.70—the best in the majors—struck out 269 batters, and walked just 46. That, in a season that he pitched in 217 innings. DeGoat indeed.

- **Ron Darling:** The best word to describe Darling's pitching career with the Mets was "steady." So steady in fact that it is hard to select one of his seasons as being appreciably better than the others. Is 16-6 with a 2.90 earned run average and 167 strikeouts in 1985 better than his 1988 season, when he went 17-9, with a 3.25 ERA and 161 strikeouts? Always overshadowed by his own teammates, Darling was quietly one of the best pitchers in the National League for much of the 1980s. Of course, fans know him today for being in the television booth, but the days he was on the mound were pretty special for the Mets and their fans. He also had one of the best pickoff moves of his generation—picking off 43 baserunners during his career—and was outstanding at fielding his position.

- **Dwight Gooden:** Let's face it, Doc Gooden is an all-time great, but it is extremely easy to select his best-ever season with the Mets, mostly because it was one of the best seasons ever by a pitcher from any team. One year before the 1986 Mets became a thing, Doc embarked on the 1985 campaign which, to say the least, was epic. Gooden went 24-4, with a 1.53 earned run average, which led the majors, as did his 268 strikeouts. Not only did Gooden win the National League Cy Young Award—duh—but he finished fourth in the MVP voting. His fastball was electric, and his curveball dropped off a table and was so incredible that instead of referring to it in baseball lingo as "Uncle Charlie," Doc's was referred to as "Lord Charles."

- **Frank Viola:** The other lefty on this list, Viola had his best seasons before arriving in New York, but in 1990 turned in a stellar campaign. That season, he went 20-12 for the Mets, posted an earned run average of 2.67, and led the National League in games started and innings pitched. He was an All-Star that season and finished third in the Cy Young voting. He is also a hometown kid, having grown up on Long Island and played college baseball at St. John's University.

- **David Cone:** Cone won a lot of games as a member of the Mets, but no season was as impressive as 1988—when the Mets won the National League East for the second time in three years. That year—Cone's first full season with the Mets—he went 20-3, with a 2.22 earned run average, and 213 strikeouts. He would go on to win 55 more games for the Mets over the next three seasons before being traded to the Toronto Blue Jays as a playoff rental. Of course, 10 years after his 1988 campaign, he won 20 games for the New York Yankees, the team for which he would also pitch a perfect game. Does he lose points for his latter misdeeds? That will be up to each individual; however the record shows that Cone was a fiery competitor and true winner during his time with the Mets.

CLOSER (Select one)

- **John Franco:** How often is your closer your team captain? Pretty much, never—although no player on the Mets was more of a captain than Franco. A kid from Brooklyn, Franco fit in very well with the Mets at Shea Stadium. A tough, scrappy New Yorker, Franco never backed down from anyone. However, it was his artistry on the mound that made him so legendary. His 1,119 games pitched are the most in National League history and the third most in major-league history. His 424 career saves ranks among the most by any relief pitcher in major-league history and remains the most by a left-hander.

- **Jesse Orosco:** No image is as vivid to Mets fans of a certain age than Orosco, on his knees, with his arms extended upwards in celebration, and his grin the size of Shea's center field. "Nothing will ever replace the moment when Jesse Orosco struck out Marty Barrett to end Game 7, and I was able to go out and jump in his arms," Carter said when he was elected to the Hall of Fame. "That was my biggest thrill." Along the way, in addition to pitching in clutch game after clutch game in the 1986 postseason, he combined with teammate Roger McDowell to be a two-headed monster out of the bullpen. They each had more than 20 saves that year. While Orosco was solid for the Mets for six seasons, he actually spent 24 seasons in the major leagues—an incredible career and show of durability. His 1,252 career-games pitched are more than any pitcher who has played the game.

- **Edwin Díaz:** Not unlike Francisco Lindor, it took Diaz a minute to fit in with the Mets—and in New York. First of all, he was acquired along with Robinson Canó from Seattle in a deal that many fans disagreed with. However, in 2018 Díaz led the majors with 57 saves—how could that be bad? Well, Díaz was not just bad, he was really bad in 2019, giving up 15 home runs, losing seven games on his own, and had an ERA of 5.59. After the COVID year of 2020 and a better 2021 season, during which Díaz saved 32 games, Díaz was given a stay by fans. Then, in 2022, he turned that stay into being the best closer in all of baseball, complete with his own theme song, thanks to Timmy Trumpet. Díaz's 32 saves in 2022 do not begin to tell the story of his season. He was unhittable in nearly every outing, did not blow a save after May, posted an earned run average of 1.31, and struck out 118 batters in just 62 innings pitched. Of course, 2023 was a lost season for Díaz—and the Mets—but the closer has high hopes he will be stronger than ever for the 2024 season.

- **Billy Wagner:** In 2006, already established as one of the best closers in baseball, Wagner arrived in New York for three very solid years with the Mets. He saved 40 games in his first year with the ballclub and posted a 2.21 earned run average. In 2007 and 2008, he saved a total of 61 games and made the All-Star team both years.

Now that you have your team, you must select your ideal batting order. I wonder—would your first-string Mets lineup defeat mine?

1. Reyes–SS

2. Beltrán–CF

3. Hernandez–1B

4. Piazza–C

5. Wright–3B

6. Strawberry–RF

7. Agee–LF

8. Alfonzo-2B

9. Seaver-P

deGrom-P
Franco-CL

LONG OVERDUE FIRSTS

THERE IS NO WAY TO JUSTIFY A BOOK ABOUT METS FIRSTS WITHOUT asking a question about a 10-foot-high baseball pitcher. Well, the actual pitcher did not stand 10-feet tall, but metaphorically he absolutely did. Who was the first Mets player to have a statue in his honor placed outside of Citi Field?

The thing is—this pitcher really never should have been on the Mets in the first place. So many strange things had to happen for that to fall into place. In 1964, Tom Seaver went 11-2 with a 1.58 ERA and 132 strikeouts for Fresno City College. In 1965, he transferred to the University of Southern California and went 10-2. The Los Angeles Dodgers drafted him in the 10th round—with the 190th overall pick. However, the Dodgers decided not to sign the young pitcher when he requested $50,000. Tom Seaver could have been a Dodger.

The following season, he was drafted once again, this time by the Atlanta Braves. A contract was signed and Seaver was reportedly excited to play for the Braves, a team he loved while growing up. However, it was illegal for a team to offer a contract to a college player if his college season had already started, and the contract was invalidated. In reality, USC had started its season, but Seaver had not played for them yet, so if someone would have pushed back, perhaps Seaver might very well have been a Brave. To make matters worse, the NCAA ruled him ineligible to play at USC because he had signed a contract with a big-league team. Lose-lose for Seaver, which would soon turn into win-win for both Seaver and the Mets. "So now to the professionals I'm an amateur and to the amateurs I'm a pro, and I'm stuck," he said years later. "My dad got in the middle of it. There was going to be some legal action somewhere because I wasn't going to be thrown in the street. I lost my scholarship and everything."

Major League Baseball decided that while Seaver could not be a member of the Braves, other teams could match the Braves' offer. Three teams—the Cleveland Indians, the Philadelphia Phillies, and the Mets—all had their names put into a hat. If Mets president George Weiss got his way, the Mets would not have even been in that hat. Years later, Mets general manager Bing Devine spoke to Peter Golenbock for his book, *Amazin'*, which was published in 2002. "Yes, [Weiss] was against taking Seaver," Devine said. "Let's be honest about it: He didn't know anything about him. And so he just said, 'We can't do it.' . . . I made a big case, and I recall it was only hours before we had to make a decision and agree to that, and George Weiss finally shook his head, I'm sure not wanting to do it, and said, 'If you people make such a big case of it, go ahead.'" Seaver could have been an Indian. He could have been a Phillie. Thankfully, he was neither.

Back to the last question about firsts; we almost let Mets history distract us—story of my life. You see the thing is, you already know who the first Mets player was to have a statue outside of Citi Field—it's Tom Seaver. For Mets fans, the 2022 unveiling happened many years too late and two years after the death of Seaver himself. His widow, Nancy, and his two daughters were on hand at the April unveiling of the 33,600-pound copper and steel likeness that was sculpted by William Behrends. Among Behrends's other baseball works are statues of Willie Mays, Willie McCovey, Tony Gwynn, and Buck O'Neil. Nancy Seaver spoke to the throng of fans on hand for the unveiling, "Hello, Tom, it's so nice to have you where you belong," she said in front of a cheering crowd.

The statue of Seaver is stunning and stands proudly right outside the entrance of Citi Field. However—and there always seems to be a however when it comes to the Mets—there is one not-so-small error on the statue. The face looks great, the pose is iconic, but the uniform is historically inaccurate. The number four in Seaver's #41 does not match the way it looked in the 1960s and 70s. Less than one month after the day it was unveiled, Behrends admitted how his mistake might have happened: "I went back and looked at my original clay model to see if the number mistake had happened in the foundry," Behrends told the website, Uni Watch. "It's not like me to miss something like that, but that's what happened. It's something I missed. That clay model, I worked on that for about 10 and a half months. I laid out the torso, laid out the uniform, and blocked in the letters. At an early stage, I know I had that little stub on the '4.' But during the process of adjusting the model, you take things off and rebuild them elsewhere. So those numbers were probably built and rebuilt five or six times in the process. And in the later part of the process, I clearly was not thinking about the number—I was thinking about other things, and I just missed it. It's embarrassing."

The incorrect numeral notwithstanding, the Seaver statue is outstanding. I remember seeing it for the first time—you never forget certain firsts.

During the 2023 season, the Mets retired Keith Hernandez's #17, making him the first player from the championship 1986 team to have his jersey retired. In August 2023, the Mets announced that they would retire the numbers of two more 1986 stars during the 2024 season— Dwight Gooden and Darryl Strawberry. Since Gooden left the Mets in 1994, 16—yes, the irony—players have worn #16. Since Strawberry left the Mets in 1990, 19 players have worn #18. So here is the big question: Who were the first players to wear numbers 16 and 18 after Gooden and Strawberry, respectively?

Following the 1990 season, when Strawberry left the Mets and headed west as the prized free agent signing of the Los Angeles Dodgers, no one wore #18 during the 1991 season. A sign of respect? Or maybe no one had the nerve to wear it so soon after Strawberry's departure. In any event, by the 1992 season Strawberry was long gone, if not forgotten, and #18 was claimed by one of the Mets' most disappointing acquisitions of a superstar ever—Roberto Alomar and Carlos Baerga notwithstanding. In 1992, the player who wore #18, and the first to wear it after Strawberry, was Bret Saberhagen.

Before Gooden ever slipped it on, #16 had a storied career with the Mets. John Stearns wore it for two seasons in the 1970s, before turning it over to teammate Lee Mazzilli, who wore it from 1976 through

1981. After wearing #64 in his rookie spring training in 1984 for the Mets, Gooden selected #16 for the regular season, the number he wore throughout his minor-league career. Gooden's last official year with the Mets was 1994, and by 1996 he was pitching for the Yankees. It wasn't until 1998, however, that the Mets issued his #16 to another player—and that player was Hideo Nomo, who wore the uni for just the one season. The important thing for the Mets, however, is that by retiring Gooden and Strawberry's numbers during the 2024 season, it officially means three of the best players from the 1986 team will be forever immortalized—16, 17, and 18.

REFERENCES

I have said this before and I will always say it: I am not sure how anyone researched and wrote any books before the internet. Yet, I hear there were quite a few books written prior to 1995! For me, there are some websites that I consider partners in my writing quest. Those include baseball-reference.com, baseball-almanac.com, mets.com, espn.com, mlb. com, SBnation.com, mentalfloss.com, and bleacherreport.com. I also was inspired by many Mets blogs—near and far—such as Amazin' Avenue, Rising Apple, Metsmerized Online, Faith and Fear in Flushing, The Ultimate Mets Database, and MetsToday. Newspapers will never die, they will just go to online archives. The ones that I went to often included the *New York Times*, *New York Daily News*, *New York Post*, *Newsday*, *The Athletic*, *USA Today*, and the *Players' Tribune*.

BIBLIOGRAPHY
Angell, Roger. *Game Time: A Baseball Companion*. Mariner Books, 2004.
Appel, Marty. *Casey Stengel: Baseball's Greatest Character*. Doubleday, 2017.
The Beatles. *The Beatles Anthology*. Chronicle Books, 2000.
Breslin, Jimmy. *Can't Anybody Here Play This Game? The Improbable Saga of the New York Mets' First Year*. Viking Press, 1963.
Golenbock, Peter. *Amazin': The Miraculous History of New York's Most Beloved Baseball Team*. St. Martin's Press, 2002.
Harrelson, Bud. *Turning Two: My Journey to the Top of the World and Back with the New York Mets*. Thomas Dunne Books, 2012.
Jackson, Reggie. *Becoming Mr. October*. Doubleday, 2013.
Okkonen, Marc. *Baseball Uniforms of the 20th Century*. Sterling, 1991.
Topel, Brett. *Miracle Moments in New York Mets History*. Sports Publishing, 2021.
———. *When Shea Was Home: The Story of the 1975 Mets, Yankees, Giants, and Jets*. Sports Publishing, 2016.

ACKNOWLEDGMENTS

This book was probably the most challenging one I have written, for various and often unforeseen reasons. Getting into a groove to write has always been a thing for me. Late nights, on the beach, at a desk, in hotel rooms, all successful options of the past that never quite felt right this time. However, I was inspired many times to make this book the best I have written, with the most inspirational moment coming on July 26, 2022.

My dad and I made the drive we had made so many times before—from my house to Citi Field to watch a Mets game. Before we made that drive, we had made the almost identical drive from my house to Shea Stadium many times. Thanks to COVID, this was the first time we were heading to a game together since the summer of 2019.

My life as a Mets fan has been a rollercoaster, just as it has been for many other fans who grew up in the 1970s. The Mets were terrible, until they started to get good in the mid-1980s, culminating with a World Series title in 1986, followed by two years of what could have been, followed by 10 or so lost years. By 1999, they had gotten good again, reaching the second World Series I can remember them in in 2000. Good years popped in and out of bad years, collapses, surprises, and more. There was 2006 and 2015 and 2016. Finally, there was 2022 when everything seemed possible.

So on that very warm July evening we were driving to Citi Field to see the first-place Mets take on the first-place New York Yankees. The two teams had not been in first place so late in the season in more than 30 years. We were ready to watch some baseball.

In the car, we always talk about a million different things, my kids—his grandchildren—my job, life in general, and, of course, the Mets. It was right around the time I was getting off of the Long Island Expressway and onto the Grand Central Parkway that I learned I had been misleading people my entire life. I say misleading because I was sure I had the correct information; it was not a case of lying or making up a story. It was simply stating a fact. I am not sure how often it had come up over the course of my life, but it had been a significant amount of times. Why was I a Mets fan? My answer always came quickly and clearly and rarely wavered from the verbatim, "When you are growing up you either follow the team your dad roots for, or you root against the team your dad roots for. Me and my dad have always been close, so I am a Mets fan like he has always been."

There didn't seem to be anything controversial about that—not on its face, not when you dig in. My dad and I have always loved the Mets and hated the Yankees. It was as simple as saying, I love Diet Coke and hate Diet Pepsi. But I was incorrect.

My dad had grown up as a fan of the New York Baseball Giants. His man was Willie Mays, who broke into the majors when my dad was nine years old. There was no Willie, Mickey, and the Duke for my dad, there was only "Say Hey" Willie Mays. However, his fandom predates Mays, who was a rookie, in the on-deck circle, when Bobby Thomson hit his shot heard 'round the world. One of my favorite days was driving me and my father to a sports card show in New Jersey so that he could meet Thomson and Ralph Branca, the man who threw the fateful pitch. I didn't tell him what we were doing until we got there. That was a fun day.

However, the Giants abandoned New York City, and my dad, when they moved to San Francisco following the 1958 season. My dad was 16, disillusioned, and without a baseball team. He has told me that the first couple of years the Giants were in San Francisco he continued to root for them. I think I would have too. So when the Mets were founded in 1962, Dad was still a Giants fan, understandably.

In 1967, he married my mom, went to serve in Vietnam, and returned home when his mother passed away in 1969. The Mets were not the highest of his priorities. I came along in 1970, and started to understand what baseball was about six years later. We always had catches, me and my dad, I always collected baseball cards, and from when I was around seven or eight, always remembered going to see the Mets play at Shea Stadium. I have vivid memories when I was a little older, maybe nine or ten, of waking up on a Sunday morning and my dad lying in bed and asking me and my sister if we wanted to go see the Mets. It was not hard to get seats at Shea in 1979 and 1980. I remember seeing Tom Seaver pitch more than once during his return in 1983, watching the team start to improve in 1984, getting really good in 1985, and then legendary in 1986. We went to games together in the late 1980s and early 1990s, when I was in college. I didn't throw as many remotes at the wall in frustration as I got older. He would always just shake his head. I do remember one game when John Franco blew a save and my dad stood up and exclaimed, "Oh, he sucks!" This is from a guy who never cursed at a time when the word *sucks* qualified. In 1996, I got married. In 2002, my son was born and, in 2008, my daughter made her debut. My Dad and I attended Mets games almost every season. We were passionate fans.

So on this July drive, as we were approaching the ballpark, he said—almost matter of factly—"You know, you're not a Mets fan because of me, I am a Mets fan because of you." How can that be, I thought to myself. "I really got into baseball because you loved it so much." How can that be, I thought to myself again. It turns out, he had drifted away from the sport he once loved and only returned when I took to the sport like a fish to water—not as a player, but as a fan. That was when Dad jumped on for the ride. And it's been the best ride I have known. Through wins, and losses, and losses, and wins, I will always maintain that I am a Mets fan because my dad is a Mets fan. I am sticking with that. Even if the reverse might be true.

There was only thing I was sure of that night; I was going to have to write about this conversation. Which I have now done. And, alas, the book is complete.

This book would not have been written, at least by me, if it was not for Niels Aaboe, senior acquisitions editor at Globe Pequot/Lyons Press. I never met Niels, but he thought enough of my past work that he offered me a contract to write this book in October 2021. He showed grace in allowing me a short extension on my deadline. I submitted the completed manuscript in October 2022, and shortly thereafter received an email from Niels saying he was in the hospital but looked forward to reading it. For various reasons, the publication date was pushed from April 2023 to February 2024, so I did not find it odd that I had not heard from Niels. In March 2023, I received a phone call from editor extraordinaire Ken Samelson, whom I had worked with in the past and have great respect for. He informed me that Niels was still on medical leave and that he would be taking over editorship of my book. I was excited to learn this, as I feel Ken is one of the best in the business and figured Niels needed more time to recover from his illness. Just weeks later, Ken informed me that Niels had passed away. I never met Niels—but I would never have written this book had it not been for him, and I dedicate this book to him. I will be forever grateful for the faith he showed in me. And I am uber-thankful to Ken and the talented team, including Chris Fischer at Lyons Press and copy editor Joshua Rosenberg, for everything they have done to care for this project.

There are always a ton of people in my corner, and the first two have been the same for more than 50 years. To my mom—and that dad I mentioned earlier—thank you always. Thank you to my wife, Emily; my son, Oliver; and my daughter, Lily—no man is as lucky as me. Thank you to Milo and Rosie and to the immortal William, who left us during the writing of this book. Thank you for the constant love and support: Melissa, Jason, Derek, Kayla, Ellen, Stephen, Abigale, David, Cooper, and Quinn. Thank you to the entire colleague body—and specifically the BLT—at Brooklyn Friends School, which was extremely supportive of me during this project. I want to center Crissy, who is such a positive and important force in my life. Special thanks to the incredible team that is so fortunate to work with me every day—Emily, Peter, and Jay. Thanks also to DG, whose biography is next on my list! There are also people in my life whom I could not imagine *not* having in my life. They span my entire journey and each one owns a piece of who I was, who I am, and who I will continue to be. I thank them for their constant, unconditional support: Shvinky, Eric and Corinne, Cree, Sam, Boyle, Elizabeth, Jon and Aaron, Karen, RJ, Rick K, Theresa, Dr. Juhel, Evan and Lisa, Jaime and Lisa. I love my family and I love my friends—well, most of them at least. I love McDonald's, Chinese food, and sushi. I love the Beatles, Billy Joel, and Bob Ross. I love chilly fall nights and driving around with no specific destination. I love writing. However, my first love—the most important first in this book—is baseball. Thank you to the New York Mets for inspiring me not only to love baseball, but to love Mets baseball. Year after year, for better or for worse, first and foremost—*Ya Gotta Believe!*